Tradition in Contemporary Furniture

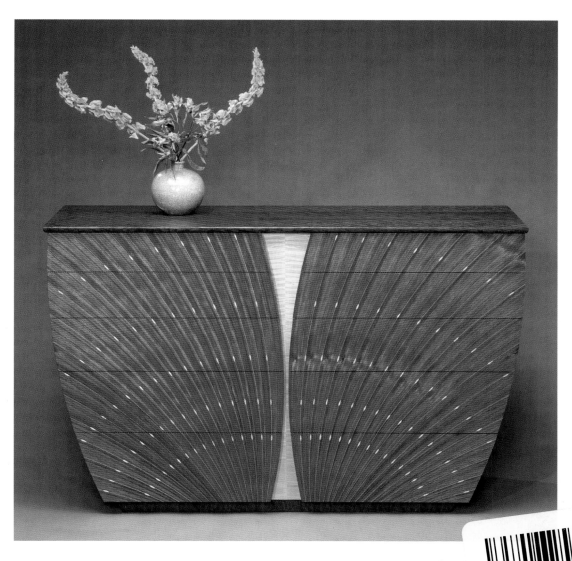

Blaise Gaston; Earlysville, VA

Lelia's Dresser 2000

Bubinga, curly maple, fishtail oak; 43"h × 65"w × 20"d

A lady's dresser for a 200-year-old home in Alexandria, Va. The house is a wonderful combination of traditional and contemporary styles. My intention with this piece is to honor Lelia, and the home where she resides.

Photo: Alan Housel

D1275545

Also in the *Furniture Studio* series:
Furniture Studio: The Heart of the Functional Arts, 1999

Yoshiaki Kato

Cabinet by Brian Newell
(see also page 20)

FURNITURE STUDIO

Tradition in Contemporary Furniture

EDITED BY
RICK MASTELLI
AND JOHN KELSEY

The FURNITURE SOCIETY
Free Union, Virginia ■ 2001

The Furniture Society is a non-profit organization
whose mission is to advance the art of furniture making by
inspiring creativity, promoting excellence, and fostering
understanding of this art and its place in society.

Series concept: Cambium Press
Produced by Image & Word
Editors: Rick Mastelli and John Kelsey
Design and layout: Deborah Fillion

Printed in Hong Kong

First printing: October 2001

Library of Congress Cataloging-in-Publication Data

Tradition in contemporary furniture / edited by Rick Mastelli and John Kelsey.
     p. cm. — (Furniture studio ; 2)
   Includes bibliographical references and index.
   ISBN 0-9671004-1-0 (alk. paper)
    1. Furniture—History—20th century.   I. Mastelli, Rick, 1949–
  II. Kelsey, John, 1946– III. Furniture Society (Free Union, Va.) IV. Series.
NK2395.T73 2001
749.2'049--dc21   2001040268

THE FURNITURE SOCIETY
PO Box 18
Free Union, VA 22940
Phone: 434-973-1488; fax: 434-973-0336
www.furnituresociety.org

Distributed to the trade by Cambium Press
PO Box 909
Bethel, CT 06801
Phone: 203-426-6481; fax: 203-426-0722
www.cambiumbooks.com

Publishing from the Heart

What I like best about the *Furniture Studio* project is the gutsy independence it represents. This beautifully produced, full-color book, the second in an on-going series, is not part of some large company's publishing program, nor is it the output of a university press. Instead, it emerges from an unlikely collaboration of furniture artists and aficionados, some of whom also have expertise as scholars, writers, editors, publishers, and organizers. The other key ingredients include a modest amount of grant money managed adroitly, a tremendous amount of low-paid and volunteer work, and long-term organizational commitment by The Furniture Society to this risky proposition. Thanks go to the Chipstone Foundation and to an anonymous foundation with an interest in the field for their continuing financial support, as well as to the authors, artists, photographers, and editorial advisors who have contributed so generously to this project.

This book is about new work by today's leading and emerging furniture artists. It is about how contemporary studio furniture has evolved from our grand furniture traditions. It is about meaning and value in contemporary furniture. Major publishers can't tackle a project like this because the audience is just too small. That leaves the field to committed individuals and organizations who've got something to say, along with the burning desire to get it said.

The first volume in the series, *Furniture Studio: The Heart of the Functional Arts,* was published in 1999. Through a smorgasbord of essays and photos, it attempted to define the contemporary studio furniture movement and map its place among the fine and decorative arts. This second volume, *Tradition in Contemporary Furniture,* has a closer focus but the same essential mission: to advance the exploration, in words and images, of our emerging field.

Everyone is familiar with the broad meanings embedded in traditional furniture: taste, comfort, wealth, and a certain sense of style. And it's not difficult to learn about its more specific vocabulary: the eighteenth-century mahogany sideboard expresses hospitality, its carved shell giving thanks for the bounty of the sea, while the curvaceous cabriole leg speaks to the quest for ideal beauty. In these ways traditional furniture makers use forms, materials, and motifs to express a variety of cultural meanings.

We're perhaps less familiar with the broad range of meanings expressed by contemporary studio furniture. The term "studio furniture" refers to work made one piece at a time or in small production runs, by individuals and small teams of artisans, for functional reasons as well as artistic ones. Today's studio furniture artists seek to widen the vocabulary of furniture and expand its range of meanings. Yet even as they press current art movements, probe newly revealed functions, and incorporate such modern materials as aluminum and acrylic, they remain within a still-unfolding tradition. Their work builds on the foundation set by the world's grand furniture cultures, even while it expresses new visions and writes new definitions. —*John Kelsey, Coeditor*

CONTENTS

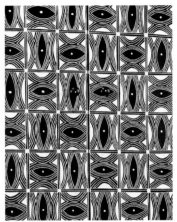

Page 106

Page 20

Page 42

Page 84

Page 72

Page 128

Decoding Studio Furniture

THE FUNDAMENTAL REALITY OF FURNITURE MAKING
IS WORK ITSELF

LOY D. MARTIN

The subtle pattern of vertical lines is Morse code that whispers, "labor of love of labor of love...." Detail of "Blanket Chest" (page 115) by Mark Del Guidice.

One of the many striking pieces in the "Furniture Gallery" sections of this volume is Mark Del Guidice's blanket chest, with its carved and milk-painted surface decoration. I have come to think of this piece as embodying a central question posed in many different ways by the entire collection of essays and images here: namely, how can studio furniture be said to bear meaning? I am looking in particular at the end panels with their regular pattern of simple long and short marks. Read as Morse code, these marks say continuously, "...labor of love of labor of love of labor of love...." Such a detail would never appear on a mass-produced piece of furniture. It would be equally surprising to find it on a painting or a piece of sculpture. Perhaps, then, this kind of decoration that turns out to harbor a hidden content has something specific to do with studio furniture. I have come to feel that a great deal of contemporary studio furniture offers encrypted messages that challenge the observer to discover their meanings. These messages are seldom as explicitly coded as Del Guidice's, but with surprising regularity they explore the themes of labor and love that he raises on his blanket chest. In doing so, they also have a lot to tell us about tradition in our form of art.

Where is tradition located? In his essay for this volume, Miguel Gomez-Ibañez asks us to see that even the most radical makers of contemporary "art furniture" are "working within a tradition," and that, conversely, the makers of

Like contemporary painters and sculptors, some furniture artists develop a personal vocabulary of line, color, and form. Detail of "Snowcheeks Hill" (page 98) by Tommy Simpson.

reproduction or "traditional furniture" are still "interpreters of our society, expressive of contemporary culture and values." This argument, though it challenges familiar ways of dividing up the field, nevertheless preserves the assumption that traditional and contemporary elements reside in the object, the piece of furniture itself.

For the most part, the other contributors to *Tradition in Contemporary Furniture* would seem to agree. In his commentary on Toronto's "Comfort" exhibition, Glenn Adamson refers us to a "chair ablaze with high orange flames" and concludes that "Clearly, traditionalism was not the watchword of this exhibition." Mark Kingwell explores the relations between functional and aesthetic values as manifested in the physical properties of furniture. Kathran Siegel finds a tradition for contemporary studio furniture makers like Tommy Simpson in the "vocabulary" they adopt from Modernist painting and sculpture. Even Scott Landis, though his tour through Shelburne Farms presents a more complex case, contrasts the more traditional or "distilled" recent work of Beeken and Parsons with their "whimsical" earlier designs.

Useful as these inquiries are, I would like to consider here a different perspective on the idea of tradition in studio furniture. I would urge that we read these mostly visual elements of style not as the actual loci of tradition but as abstract signifiers, as products of the imagination that require interpretation before we can know what

real relations to the past they indicate. To do this, we must look beyond the furniture itself toward a more basic reality that it interprets. In short, I think that, more often than not, studio furniture finds ways to communicate something about the actual work its makers do to create it.

The Meaning of Work

Del Guidice has already pointed to this more basic reality by making his blanket chest explicitly into a coded field of signs. The piece literally speaks *about* his labor in making it, and, as we shall see, it expresses a subtle ambivalence toward that labor. In places, Gomez-Ibañez himself seems to relocate furniture tradition prior to the finished piece in the conditions of its production. In pointing out elements of tradition in

Peter Handler's work, he turns to a description of Handler's workshop:

> Peter Handler spends his days in a small workshop in northwest Philadelphia, assisted by an apprentice who is the latest of many young furniture makers employed and trained in his shop, a number of whom have gone on to start their own furniture-making businesses.

In short, the fundamental reality of furniture making is work itself, the process of making each piece and the specific material and economic con-

For the artist, the difficulties and rewards of doing the work can be more valuable than the furniture itself. Jere Osgood (pages 72–83) clamps up the shell for one of his Shell Desks.

ditions in which it is made. The finished piece is a part of that reality, but for each moment the maker contemplates that final product, he or she spends dozens or even hundreds of hours enacting its production. The importance of this reality emerges at the very beginning of Jere Osgood's reflections on his own career. He tells us that the "life of a piece" has three phases:

> ...first is designing the piece, second is making the piece, and third is responding to it. The difficulty and the rewards of the second phase are very important

to me. I participate in the making of the piece, and that experience can't be sold. You can't give it away. But to me it's the reason for doing it. In many ways it's more valuable than the piece itself.

I would argue that the value attached to this "second phase," the "making of the piece," by the maker, by the consumer, and by the economic community at large, generates a widely variable language for the many complex meanings of studio furniture.

Gomez-Ibañez reminds us, in the example of Peter Handler, that however wide the differences may be among the styles of studio furniture, the materials and tools that we as makers use or the ideologies that we serve, the *ways that we work* remain remarkably similar, remarkably traditional. To say that furniture is "studio furniture" is to say that it is made in a small workshop, where anywhere from one to five people produce useful objects, either one at a time or in small batches. If the shop is a one- or two-person enterprise, each worker usually does all tasks, and specialization is minimal. In larger shops we may find more division of labor and more hierarchical sorting of tasks, but in general the principal of the shop is fully engaged in the fabrication of the product. If the business grows to the point where wage labor effects all production while owners and managers only manage, it has moved into a different form of economic organization, and the product can no longer usefully be called studio furniture. For the businesses of Thomas Moser or George Nakashima in his later career to claim some of the attractive sentimental attributes of "custom design" or "hand craftsmanship" is no more than a marketing strategy. The *way of working* in these enterprises has moved away from the small shop to the factory mode.

Labors of Love

The practice of labor in a small shop can meaningfully be called a traditional practice. Drive through any region zoned for light industry in any major urban area and you will see countless small shops: machinists, upholsterers, refinishers, cabinet shops, custom milling shops, metal spinners—the list could go on. Their mode of organization has a history and an ideology, a set of ideas and beliefs—even feelings—that appear self-evident. This is what we mean when we say that such work is traditional. Tradition is a set of expectations about a given activity that tells us what is familiar about that activity, what seems most "natural" to it. Tradition is what we are most inclined to assume. We assume that the hands and bodies of the workers in a small shop are somehow close to the work and that much of the work is both physically demanding and manually skilled. We assume that the proprietor understands his shop's production in all its details and that he probably possesses the skills of his assistants even if he seldom uses them. We may expect both minimum and maximum levels of education among those who work there. We probably look for a kind of blue-collar environment but with a difference from the environment of a factory—perhaps more comradeship, a less rule-regulated set of relations and conditions. We expect these businesses to be profitable—but not too profitable. We look here for people who work hard and expect to be decently paid for their work but who do not stress ways to multiply or, in the current buzz word, "exponentiate" their profits. All of these assumptions and expectations form part of the tradition of small shop labor.

Studio furniture shops are small shops but often with an important difference, and that's where the complexity of the furniture maker's relation to tradition comes in. The chief purpose of working in a traditional small shop is to make a living, something which is notoriously difficult to do making studio furniture. This separates furniture making from other practices of small shop working because it requires a source of motivation beyond the desire to make money. Such motivation varies widely from maker to maker, but the essential point here is that it is seldom, if ever, simple or free of conflict. And this observation takes us back to Mark Del Guidice's chest.

By blending the two phrases "labor of love" and "love of labor" into a continuous syntactic serpent with its tail in its mouth, Del Guidice has captured the seamless ambivalence of the studio furniture maker's struggle with tradition. The tradition of labor in small shops has little to say about love. Love comes into the equation, perhaps as an interloper from the artist's studio next door, to fill in the economic deficiencies of furniture making. If you can't make a living as eas-

Karen Mouch

Whatever the medium or the idea content, the ways that furniture makers work are remarkably similar. Peter Handler (pages 43 and 112) assembles an aluminum chair frame.

ily making furniture as a small shop owner "traditionally" does, you must be doing it "for love." But for love of what or whom? It is each maker's answer to this question that so often involves ambivalence or outright contradiction and that will ultimately yield the keys to interpreting the furniture itself.

When we say that something is a "labor of love" we generally mean that it is unlike ordinary labor. I cook a delicious meal for my wife and myself and she declares it a "labor of love." That means there was something extra in my work that led to something extra in the meal that gave it a special "aura," to snatch a famous term from Walter Benjamin, the cultural historian. That something extra is love, the kind of specialness we might infer from the beautiful chest by Blaise Gaston that graces the cover of this volume. Gaston calls that piece "Lelia's Dresser," and by that he seems to tell us that the unique "aura" of the piece arises from the fact that it was made *for* someone who is more to him than just another customer. In short, it is a labor of love.

Love can, of course, be directed at many objects other than people, and the "labor of love" side of the equation can encompass work that stems from the love of certain materials (e.g., beautiful wood or stone), a historical period, a political principle, a geographical place, or, certainly, from the love of Art. The list could

What is the object of a labor of love? Detail of "Lelia's Dresser" (cover and page 1) by Blaise Gaston.

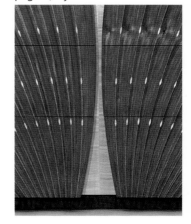

The two- or three-person workshop can produce furniture of real beauty and strength in prodigious quantity. Studio furniture maker Sam Maloof (see also page 44) lays out the back spindles on a run of rockers.

be much longer, but the point is that whatever we insert as the object of love, the message is the same, and it goes something like this: "I have labored to make this object. I have not done it entirely for the money, for that was not enough, and I have not done it just to have work to do. I have done it for Lelia." Or, "I have done it to express the essence of the folk art of Kentucky." Or, "I have done it to honor the soul of a tree." It was a labor of love.

In a certain sense, the labor of love, as described here, is an expression of ambivalence about the labor itself, a measure of the extra element of motivation the maker needs to do the work. Some studio furniture makers—perhaps those with advanced educations or more privileged social backgrounds—may entertain conflicting thoughts and feelings about working each day with their hands and bodies. These thoughts, whether consciously or not, invoke "traditional" stereotypes of daily shop labor and the implica-

tions about social class these stereotypes carry with them. For others, ambivalence about traditional forms of small shop labor stems from its inefficiency, the relation between work and time that is so much more efficiently exploited in the organization of mass production that dominates our culture (and the furniture industry) at large. Redefining studio furniture as art may be an expression of the maker's uncertainty about whether the sheer quantity of labor necessary to produce a given piece is justified.

And so we come full circle to the "labor of love" as one antidote to difficulties with the furniture maker's "love of labor." As Jere Osgood implies, the love of the work itself has to be there in some measure, but that love, in different degrees for different makers, comes with a burden of conflict or ambivalence. What Mark Del Guidice has recalled to us with his blanket chest is that the love of making furniture and the need to express, deny, or repair the deficiencies in that love is a seamless tradition of our practice. Moreover, holding this perception in mind can give us a powerful engine for interpreting a wide range of studio furniture.

What the "Nail Cabinet" Says

Take the "Nail Cabinet," for example. Some love it and some hate it, but all seem to agree that Garry Knox Bennett's "Nail Cabinet" was an important statement in the history of studio furniture. Writing recently about the cabinet (in Bennett's book, *Made in Oakland*), Arthur C. Danto elegantly repeats and enlarges the standard interpretation. He says that "by driving a nail into an exemplar of high craft…Bennett repudiated the very idea of purity in the art of woodworking." Danto finds the source of that idea of purity in Modernist aesthetics as articulated by Clement Greenberg and therefore uses it to locate Bennett's cabinet in the history of art. The nail, then, is a desecration, and it was bent over "for emphasis." Perhaps Danto should have stopped there and said no more about the nail, but instead he disturbs the neatness of his own interpretation by elaborating:

> For emphasis, he bent the nail over as would an inept or indifferent carpenter, leaving the marks of hammer blows in the cabinet's impeccable padouk surface.

But what do inept carpenters and the marks of hammer blows have to do with the history of art? Do they not perhaps have more to do with the history of work? And do we not have in this cabinet, more perhaps even than a desecration of art, an uncomfortable coexistence of two vastly divergent traditions of working with wood?

The standard interpretation of "Nail Cabinet" requires, at the very least, that the cabinet itself be, as Danto says, an "exemplar of high craft." But anyone who has seen the actual cabinet is surely bound to doubt this premise. It is a competent and nicely designed bit of small shop furniture making, nothing more. Bennett knows how to work wood. If he had wanted to make a cabinet with the fine handwork of a Krenov cabinet he could have done so, perhaps making the act of driving a nail into it that much more shocking. But the piece is sufficient for what it signifies. Though its details are rendered with standard router bits and its fit and finish are even occasionally sloppy, the piece adequately indicates a construction process that is relatively slow and painstaking.

The nail, on the other hand, signifies a kind of labor that literally happens in a different time scale. For the framer, speed is the primary value—one piece of wood is joined to another in an instant with a hammer stroke—and the occasional carelessness of speed has been encrypted here in the bent nail and the hammer marks in the wood. These details function as a code, just as if they were Morse code. The nail, a fastener, fastens nothing here; it only reports how quickly it was driven in contrast with how slowly the cabinet itself had to be built. We know it has this coding function because of the way it contrasts with another coded message built into the cabinet itself: the joinery of Bennett's drawer construction. Finger joints also are a way of fastening one piece of wood to another, but by a more labor-intensive method that bespeaks that "other world" of working wood in a furniture studio.

Why does Bennett use visible joinery in a cabinet style that historically calls for all end grain to be hidden? Danto thought the point was to break a stylistic rule. Is it not more obvious that visible joinery reveals and celebrates the maker's skill and painstaking, while concealed joinery places the work of construction "out of sight, out of mind?" These finger joints appear through the drawer fronts because that places them in the same plane with the nail. Any doubt that the nail chiefly refers to the processes of joining wood parts should be dispelled by Bennett himself who tells us "I wanted to make a statement that I thought people were getting a little too goddam precious with their technique. I think tricky joinery is just to show, in most instances, you can do tricky joinery." Together, the nail and the "tricky joinery" of the drawers encode a dialectical opposition in the relation of work to time.

In the end, "Nail Cabinet" is about work, about the time and skill it takes to make a basic cabinet in a furniture workshop and about Bennett's ambivalence toward that tradition of work. It is important to invoke his ambivalence, not his antipathy. For thirty years he has been a partner in a traditional small industrial enterprise, a metal-plating shop, where success is measured by the speed and efficiency of production. In his own choice of furniture making, he has found, in a sense, a middle ground between that traditional form of work and the practice of "fine art" with which his career began. His persona is that of the no-nonsense-artist for whom the effete connotations of "fine art" become demystified by gestures of down-to-earth, even working class, iconoclasm. Such iconoclasm is ambivalent in its very nature. It looks upon care, refinement, and the lavish expenditure of labor in the arts with an inseparable combination of affection and contempt. And is not studio furniture the perfect medium in which to express this ambivalence? Caught between its own contradictory traditions of humble functionality and decorative excess, studio furniture stands in an ideal position to pose the underlying value questions about how to organize labor and materials in the practice of making.

All of these issues, both the personal and the more widely political, have been encoded in the "Nail Cabinet," and if we look beyond this one piece to the full range of Garry Knox Bennett's work, we can see them expanded through a kind of alternation, between complex difficult pieces that announce themselves as the fruit of great and careful labor and pieces that seem almost "tossed off," as casual experiments in simple visual forms. We might say that, at times, Bennett can indulge freely in the love of making in itself while at others his work tells us only of his fascination with an idea or a shape in space. His work mixes, in other words, the love of labor with labors of love, and the mix oscillates over time.

Garry Knox Bennett's "Nail cabinet" (detail above; overall view on page 97) finds a middle ground between the work of making and the practice of fine art.

Surface and Depth

Both the "Nail Cabinet" and Mark Del Guidice's blanket chest can be seen as a kind of palimpsest, a surface on which the ancient writing of a tradition of work has been erased and replaced by a new message in the old code of transcribed labor. Perhaps this is why so much of studio furniture focuses on the surface that first confronts a viewer. Milk paint decorates the surface plane. Visible joinery emerges from it. A nail disrupts it. For many of our finest furniture makers, from Kristina Madsen to John Cederquist to Silas Kopf, the surface, to twist McCluhan, is the message. But is this "encryption" a universal? Does it somehow define studio furniture? Perhaps it's too early to answer this question, and certainly if we look always for furniture's coded message on a frontal surface we will often be frustrated. A currently dominant feature need not be the defining feature of a genre. Still, the idea that studio furniture encodes complex thoughts and feelings about the working practice of its makers opens a rich vein of interpretation for the work of many fine and thoughtful makers.

Look at the innovative router joinery in a Sam Maloof chair. Does it not express his lifelong struggle to prove that, with sufficient ingenuity and intensity of effort, the two- or three-person shop can produce furniture of real beauty and strength in prodigious quantity? This claim is surely at the center of Maloof's pride. It is the reason he has stayed in the shop, maintained his love of the labor itself and resisted the opportunities to become the CEO of an ever-expanding furniture manufacturing business. When we interpret something like a distinctive bit of joinery, we do so by asking questions about it, and we proceed to refine our questions with the interpretations they yield. (This is what philosophers call the hermeneutic circle.) Maloof's obvious love of the process of furniture making amounts to a full identification of the self with the work and might lead us to ask of other makers how far this kind of identification has "settled in" or to what degree a kind of lingering alienation manifests itself in either a denial of labor or an excessively urgent display of it.

To illustrate the full and rich blending of the maker's identity with the process of working itself, we need look for no more emblematic example than the career of James Krenov. Krenov is probably not our most talented designer of furniture, but he is indisputably a great and fully integrated worker at the bench. That bench is his unvarying station, the spiritual center he has never abandoned. His books have titles like "The Fine Art of Cabinet*making*" or "James Krenov: *Worker* in Wood," and, in both his writing and his teaching, he has repeatedly argued that the character of great furniture is determined by the state of mind in which the maker approaches each moment of his or her labors. There can be no doubt of Krenov's belief that this "quietness"—the integration of the person with the tools and materials and action of making an object—displays itself in the object itself. This is what he calls the maker's "fingerprints" on the work, literally the faint marks of planes and chisels and knives properly used. In the terms of our questions here, these physical marks iterate yet another kind of coded message, one that Krenov believes can be not only seen but felt by the sensitive observer.

To the uninitiated eye, most pieces by James Krenov appear to be the result of less labor than is actually the case. In the work of some of his students, however, the encoding of work/time for the eye of the beholder tends to be more aggressive, as we find in the carved work and parquetry of Brian Newell in this volume or the embossed patterns of Timothy Coleman or the marquetry of Craig Vandall Stevens, Zivko Radenkov, and others. Indeed, if we look closely at work produced at the College of the Redwoods under Krenov's tutelage, we discover a full spectrum of coded labor from the frankness of those who use the literal surface of their pieces to signify the days and months of their efforts to others whose encryption is more esoteric.

In "Box" by Jeff Shallenberger, for example, an abstract pattern of panels on the surface reveals, only with the help of a secret magnetic opening device, numerous drawers opening in all directions. These drawers are joined with dozens of tiny dovetails, entailing literally thousands of hand-saw and chisel strokes. The dovetails are a coded message that must literally be opened before it can be read.

"Komposition #7: Window into Broken Dreams" by J.P. Vilkman carries an even more arcane message, this time "behind closed doors." Those who fully understand drawer construction know that the test of a perfectly fitted drawer is to push it into the closed position by applying a

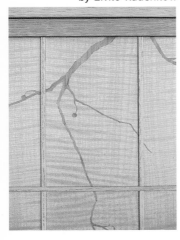

Beautiful details signify days and perhaps weeks of careful effort. Above, detail of "Cabinet" (page 20) by Brian Newell. Below, detail of "Cabinet," (pages 61 and 63) by Zivko Radenkov.

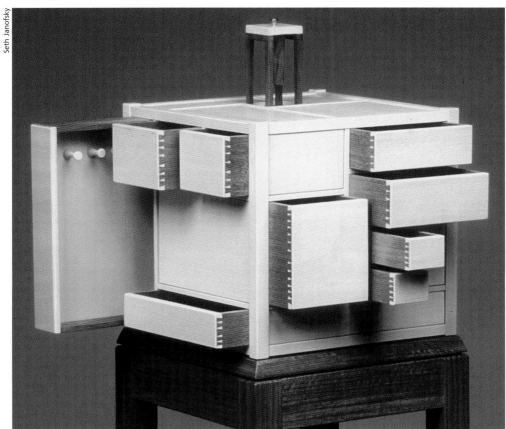

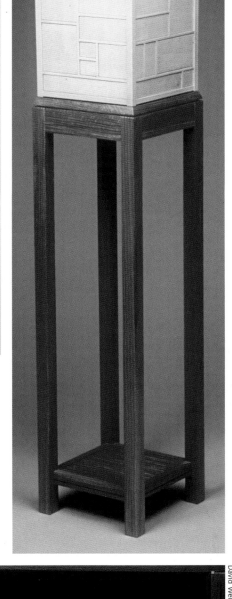

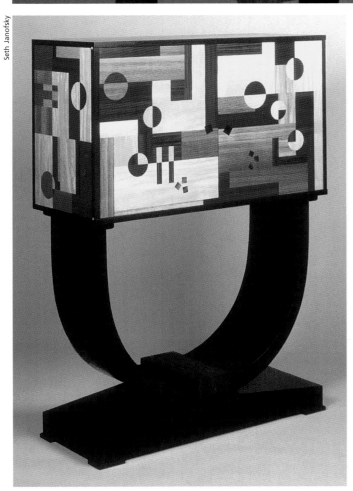

Hidden messages. In "Box" by Jeff Shallenberger (right and above) an abstract pattern of panels on the surface reveals, only with the help of a secret magnetic opening device, numerous drawers opening in all directions. "Komposition #7: Window into Broken Dreams" by J.P. Vilkman (left and below) carries an even more arcane message, this time "behind closed doors."

light force to any corner of the drawer front. To make many drawers that pass this test every time requires great and slow care in the fitting of each one. Vilkman has placed all of the pulls near the corners of his drawers in order to announce that all of the drawers should be operated from those telling points.

The Value of Anxiety

The advantage of examining the work of James Krenov in the context of his students' work is that it allows us to observe a range of urgency or anxiety regarding the relation of the signifier to the signified in the labor-intensive style taught in Krenov's school. Anyone who wants to see that relationship spelled out in detail need only read Craig Vandall Stevens' book, *Creating Coffee Tables: An Artistic Approach*. There, he lucidly takes us through every step of making the simplest of coffee tables by the method Krenov teaches. The chasm between the apparent simplicity of the signifier (the table itself) and the unseen signified (the process of its making) has been bridged by this fine book. But such a book

Detail of "10,000 Dreams" (page 33) by Brad Engstrom.

must in part be motivated by a concern that mere observation will not lead the table's "reader" to decode correctly its message about the maker's labors.

When anxiety enters into the encryption of work in studio furniture, the stylistic code may diverge in many directions to express it. Several of these pathways lead to the question, "What gives studio furniture its value?" When anxiety over this question runs low, we may find the studio piece not easily distinguished from one that could be mass produced, as in Timothy Philbrick's "Club Chair" (page 22). But when the maker feels that an overt claim must be made, or an explanation offered, as to what gives value to the work, one solution is to make large quantities of time manifest in the piece itself. A case in point would be Brad Engstrom's "10,000 Dreams," the surface of which is entirely carved with "30,000 hand-colored notches." Engstrom tells us the number in an artist's statement where he also describes furniture making as an "obsession."

For a contrasting instance of surface carving that does not read as "obsessive" or anxiety driven, we might consider the recent work of Kristina Madsen. Madsen's study of traditional carving in the South Pacific required years of living with a master carver there and yielded a full integration of the method of work into the personal identity of the maker. Accordingly, the work, though based on the practice of repetition, never seems designed to promote anxious energy as the basis of value. Rather, her furniture expresses a peaceful and comforting interaction

Furniture artists struggle to achieve a full integration of the method of work into their personal identity. Above: "Low Chest of Drawers" (1999) by Kristina Madsen, padauk, dyed pearwood, chakte kok, silk. Left: Madsen demonstrates the decorative carving technique she learned from a Fijiian master.

between two cultural traditions of work, an exchange that she has symbolized even beyond the work itself by returning a gift of Western carving tools to her principal teacher in Fiji.

If uneasiness over manual shop labor as the basis of studio furniture can be expressed through an excessive inscription of that labor in the physical piece itself, more often we find an opposite strategy. That opposite tack is somehow to encode the minimalizing of labor. To understand what this means, we need to recall that, when we speak here of labor, we are speaking of a certain kind of traditional labor: the making of useful objects in small shop production. The traditional artist's studio stands outside this tradition and avoids many of the cultural stereotypes of wage labor, however demanding the actual physical activity of making art or sculpture may be. Hence, we

should probably recognize the widespread attempt to redefine studio furniture as fine art as a kind of "class shift." In Tommy Simpson's work, for example, the piece of furniture itself virtually disappears, becoming little more than the textured canvas for a painting. And Jenna Goldberg tells us explicitly of her "Tall Cabinet" (page 124) that she was "interested in the way different patterns affect each other, as in the difference between the inside and outside of the cabinet."

Techniques and Materials

The redefinition of furniture as art or sculpture is only the currently most fashionable form of the more general gesture of coding furniture as if it were something else. But there are other strategies. Timothy O'Neill tells us that, in his shop, he works both wood and metal. Implicitly, he locates these activities as "hard" forms of work. By contrast, "shapes can *easily* be mocked up with stiff paper to create the desired form" (emphasis mine). In making his "Origami Table," O'Neill does the hard work of shaping and joining the wood into his table base, yet its chosen shape *represents* work in the other, "easier,"

Detail of "Origami Table" (page 127) by Timothy O'Neill.

medium of paper. The folding of paper to make origami, moreover, moves the maker's work out of the Western tradition of the workshop and into a Japanese tradition, one that carries implications of refinement, delicacy, discernment, and effortless technique. The same kind of analysis can be used to interpret works like Michael Hurwitz's "Shelf in Nest," where traditions of fine basket making "lighten" our sense of what is involved in making a set of shelves, a "traditional" woodworking project.

In general, the use of specialized techniques "detraditionalizes" the observer's perception of significant labor in studio furniture. What we see in the work of Michael Hosaluk or Mark Sfirri is the turning, not so much the construction of the desk or bench. In pieces by Clifton Monteith (page 106) or Randy Holden we focus on the mastery of rustic materials. Priscilla Cypiot combines wood and metal in structures for furniture, but she writes that "the ability to pattern the metal transforms it into an expressive medium and a potentially powerful narrative device." Special technique "transforms" furniture into something else, something like a literary genre.

Engagement Unlocks the Code

The idea of reading studio furniture as a wide array of encrypted messages about the real practice of making furniture is, in the end, just a metaphor. It's a metaphor that reminds us of the need to interpret this work as we respond to it. Does it grant us special access to the makers' intentions? Does it give us a key to evaluate their work? Perhaps not. Rich Tannen may have combined cedar shakes with polished white oak in his "Outdoor Bench" merely because he found the combination of textures pleasing. But if we observe that the two materials refer symbolically to two different traditions of building with wood, the bench yields a field of associations that pulls us deeper into its mysterious materiality.

This essay attempts to begin assembling a cipher—or an encryption template—for understanding the many meanings embedded in the work we do in our studios. It proceeds from an implicit theory. The theory begins with Jere Osgood's observations about the importance of the "second phase" of a piece's creation. It begins, in other words, with the assumption that the studio furniture maker can never dissociate his or her designs from concerns about how those designs *can be made* into real furniture. Going further, it assumes that, in most cases, the maker devotes considerably more time and mental energy to the actual making than to either the abstract imagining of the piece or the contemplation of it once it is finished. This is why studio furniture always has a certain "aura" that distinguishes it from factory-produced furniture. Because in all that 'time while the mind is engaged directly, and often fiercely, with the material process of the piece's becoming, the mind is thinking and feeling and evolving. It is

Thomas Brummett

Combining furniture making with other traditions, such as sculpture or carpentry or basket making, gives additional perspective on the work that goes into furniture. Michael Hurwitz's "Shelf in Nest" (1997).

Detail of "Adirondack-style Buffet" (page 119) by Randy Holden.

Detail of "Entry Table" (page 25) by Priscilla Cypiot.

Detail of "Outdoor Bench" (page 120) by Rich Tannen.

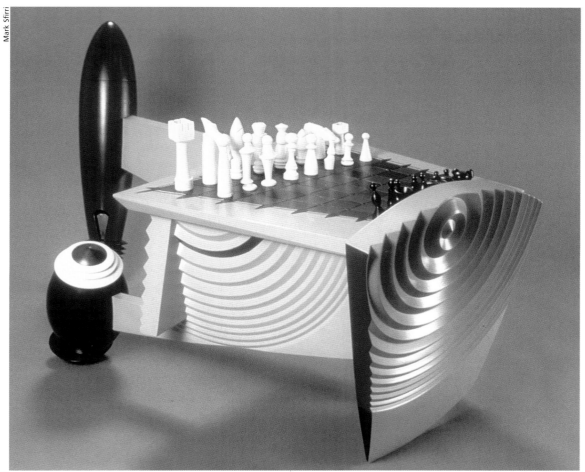

Mark Sfirri

Specialized techniques such as turning or metal casting shift attention away from the traditional. "Chessed" (1997) by Mark Sfirri, Michael Hosaluk, Steve Loar, and their students at Arrowmont School of Arts and Crafts.

interpreting its own labor and the labor of the body it directs. It is, as Krenov would say, "composing" the piece at hand, and all that the maker is thinking and feeling about the work itself is also feeding forward into the next design, the next piece.

These are long hours of engagement. They are hours and days and weeks during which the mind progresses in an atmosphere of some stress, some questioning, and doubt. My theory here says that the rich mixture of our love of the labor with the other motivations or "loves" that lead us to that labor, along with all of our doubts, anxieties, and uncertainties, cannot be withheld from the actual objects we make. I am drawing here on theories of the mind that regard all thought, even unconscious thought and feeling, as "structured like a language." This means that our individual thoughts exist for us only insofar as they can be coded. And when we are immersed in the "second phase" of creating fur-

niture, the codes that allow us to think and respond to our work tend to appear inscribed in the work itself.

In theory the fully decrypted representation of a given piece could be entirely held in the private domain of the maker, intelligible to no one else. More often, though, it will be writ large in the piece itself and accompanied by a key to unlock the code for any observer attentive enough to use it. The key will have a psychological axis, but it will also have an historical axis, a referral of thoughts about work to the broader cultural traditions that define the maker's mode of working.

Starting from these ideas, I have searched the field of contemporary furniture and found a few interesting makers who seem to be speaking with a special clarity through their work. The volume before us offers a wealth of fascinating furniture to question and some articulate questioners. Let us turn the pages together and look further. ∎

Furniture Gallery

PART ONE

The best new studio furniture
selected by The Furniture Society

It takes a society to raise a show like this. These pictures were chosen from more than a thousand slides submitted by 270 Furniture Society members. The jury was the five *Furniture Studio* editorial advisors (see page 4), plus this book's coeditors. We were most impressed with the creativity, expertise, and commitment of the makers who submitted such fine and diverse work. You'll see in this gallery (and in its continuation on page 106) all kinds of furniture forms, functions, styles, materials, ideas, and approaches—the best recent work from those whose mastery has become familiar and essential to the field, as well as from less established makers, whose bold ventures invigorate our expectations for studio furniture.

Commonly, an exhibition theme challenges submissions and guides selections. In this case the call to "send us your best work completed since the beginning of 1998" suggested little in the way of an agenda beyond building on the gallery presentation of the first book of this series (*Furniture Studio: The Heart of the Func-*

Brian Newell
Atsugi, Kanagawa, Japan

Cabinet 2000
East Indian rosewood, pearwood,
African ebony; stand: wenge
60"h × 45"w × 20"d
(detail on pages 2–3)
Photo: Yoshiaki Kato

tional Arts, 1999). The first cull, then, was the membership's self-selection; the extent and quality of the turnout is a measure of the evolving character of The Furniture Society itself.

Selecting work for exhibition does not usually involve more than three jurors. The seven of us represent various points of view, reflective of the Society's constituency. Among us are represented the maker, designer, teacher, historian, collector, curator, writer, editor, publisher, and photographer, all with a long-held commitment to the field of studio furniture. We took turns wearing each of our several hats in discussions throughout the two days we devoted to reviewing the slides. Out of those discussions, the theme of this book gelled.

The combination of traditional and contemporary ideas, a tension that achieves harmony in the best studio furniture, is evident throughout the work you see here. You can read about it in the accompanying makers' statements, as well as in the book's essays, which frame this gallery.

—*Rick Mastelli, Coeditor*

James Schriber
New Milford, CT

Double Chest with Stand 2000
Macassar ebony, pomele sapele,
mahogany, cast bronze pulls
75"h × 36"w × 15"d
Photo: John Kane

Timothy S. Philbrick
Narragansett, RI

Club Chair 1999
Cherry, ash, calf skin
38"h × 33"w × 31"d
Photo: Ric Murray

Rick Wrigley
Provincetown, MA

Sideboard with Hummingbirds 1999
Mahogany solids; figured anegre, pomele
sapele, and marquetry veneers; ebony
toes; negro marquina marble top
40"h × 46"w × 22"d
Photo: Dean Powell

Ted Blachly
Warner, NH

Cheval Glass 2000
East Indian rosewood,
satinwood, brass, mirror
64" h × 28" w × 24" d

*I'm going for a calm and
elegant feel in my furniture.
Also a touch of sensualness
with the shaping.*

Photo: Dean Powell

Priscilla Cypiot
Oakland, CA

Entry Table 1999
Peroba, aluminum
32"h × 54"w × 8"d

I love combining wood and metal in my work. The obvious textural contrasts enhance the appreciation of both materials. But the ability to pattern the metal transforms it into an expressive medium and a potentially powerful narrative device.

Photo: Ira Schrank

Paul Henry
Carlsbad, CA

Cromwell 2000
Beeswing and burled eucalyptus veneer, walnut,
white oak, gold leaf, found objects
79"h × 18.5"w × 11"d

*Having once thought of Cromwell as an intolerant reformer, I have come
to see something heroic in his leadership "interregnum" — keeping time
until the restoration of King Charles II. Thus he is depicted as a clock,
with just a hint of a crown. Based on the American clock by John Welch.*

Pepin the Short 2000
White oak, basswood, silver leaf
37"h × 11.5"w × 10.5"d

*Pepin is also a royal portrait: First Carolingian king of the Franks and father
to Charlemagne. He tapers up from the base, rising like a short cathedral
into a gothic arch above the linenfold panels, topped with a silver crown.
Also in the series: Elizabeth I, John, William, Mary, Louis le Michelin.*

Photos: David Harrison

Linda Sue Eastman
Winona, MN

Black and Gray Chaise 1999
Handtooled and dyed leather, bent laminated birch
37"h × 60"w × 24"d

Paisley Chaise 1999
Handtooled and dyed leather, suede, bent laminated birch
37"h × 60"w × 37"d

I find as a designer/maker that creating is not an unaccompanied experience. From the present I look to contemporary makers. From the past I am guided by an idea so well expressed by William Morris concerning craftsmen: "Memory and imagination help him as he works. Not only his own thoughts, but the thoughts of the men of past ages guide his hands; and, as a part of the human race, he creates."

Kurt Nielsen
Belmont, NC

Minotaur Console 2000
African satinwood, mahogany, pomele sapele, 14k gold
32"h × 38"w × 19"d

*Hand-carved, secret compartments, solid gold horns and nose
rings, adjustable shelving inside.*

Photo: David Ramsey

Jon Brooks
New Boston, NH

One Voice 1998
Maple, curly maple, acrylic,
color pencil, lacquer
64"h × 45"w × 45"d

*A back-to-back two-seater carved
frame (body) from maple tree
branches covered with acrylic
paint and color pencil. Curly
maple seats and backs carved.*

Photo: Dean Powell

Craig Vandall Stevens
Sunbury, OH

Dame Granadillo 1999

Granadillo, fiddleback maple, spalted maple,
bubinga, spalted pear, brass with patina
50"h × 28"w × 13"d

*A commissioned cabinet exploring form and gentle curves. The
rich colorful grain of the granadillo works well in large expanses.
Great care was taken not to distract from the grain with subtle
curves in the doors and legs. The medallion and forged brass
pulls become the initial focal point without being overpowering.
Interior veneered in bright fiddleback maple is a bit of a surprise.
The drawers are suspended and share a common drawer pull.
The shelves are adjustable.*

Photo: Stephen Webster

John Dodd
Canandaigua, NY

Magazine Screen 1999

Mahogany, madrone veneer, glass shelves,
absolute black granite base
83"h × 11"w × 4"d; base: 19.5"w × 11"d

*This piece serves as a room divider as it
provides three places to display precious
objects and hidden areas in which to store
magazines and/or books — a solution to the
problem of unsightly and unorganized
piles of magazines.*

Photo: Woody Packard

Tom Loeser
Madison, WI

Multiple Complications 3 1999
Wenge, mahogany, paint
50" h × 34" w × 21" d

Collection of Milwaukee Art Museum, Purchase, Doerfler Fund.

Photo: Bill Fritsch

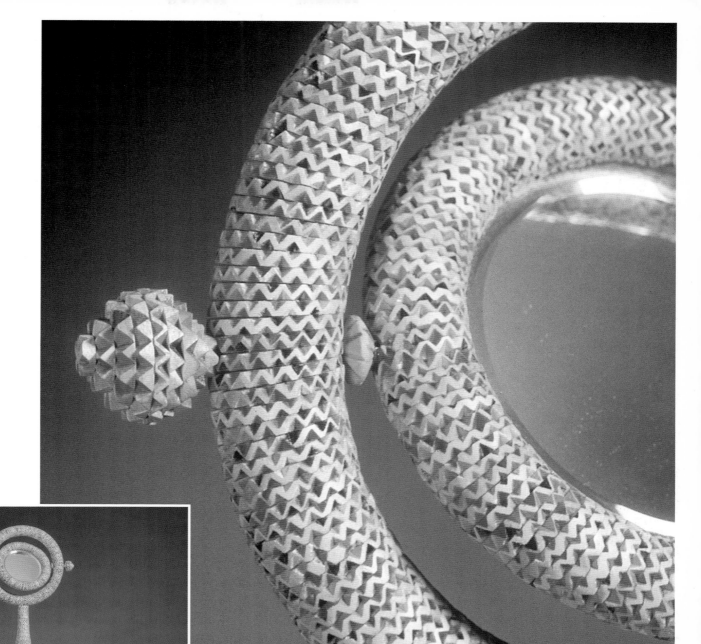

Brad Engstrom
Verona, WI

10,000 Dreams 1999

Basswood, pastels, lacquer
54"h × 25"w × 12"d

*This piece is repetition exponentiated. It's a tribute
to my obsession with making furniture. It is an
organized field of micro spaces for someone else's
obsessions. There are thirty-two drawers, five hidden
compartments, and 30,000 hand-colored notches.*

Photo: Bill Fritsch/Harper-Fritsch

Drew Nener
Montreal, Quebec

Orbital 1999

Sapele, cork, aluminum, glass
31"h × 72"w × 33"d

The objective was to create an enticing, ultra-functional computer desk designed to stand alone in an open-plan office. I've combined an innovative, kidney-shaped cork desktop with the ergonomics of a lowered keyboard tray and the convenience of integral cable-management features.

Photo: Drew Nener

Phillip Tennant
Indianapolis, IN

House of Hip-Hop 2000
Re-sawn parallam beam

This tall three-door CD cabinet owes much of its inspiration to the rural midwest landscape's worn and abandoned grain elevators and silos.

Photo: Patrick Bennett

Timothy Mowry
Annapolis, MD

Storage Cabinet 2000
Cherry, cocobolo, maple
36"h × 36"w × 20"d

*A Chinese burial shroud I saw at a museum exhibit inspired the inlay
for these door panels. Hundreds of tiny jade tiles were stitched together
with silk threads to form a body-shaped cover for the deceased.
Each tile had ribbons crossed over their center to form an "X" pattern.
I made the inlay slightly proud to give the panels some texture.*

Photo: PRS Associates

Daniel Peoples
Lake Ann, MI

Stand Tall 1 & 3 1999
Two 2x4s, aspen, enamel, clear
lacquer, upholstery tacks
78"h × 18"w × 20"d

*The inspiration behind this piece was to take mundane materials
and turn them into art. The materials of choice were as follows:
2x4s from Home Depot, 12 board feet of aspen, upholstery
tacks, Wal-Mart brand spray paint, and a clear lacquer top coat.
The studs form the frame, while the slates are aspen.*

Photo: Clifton Monteith

Kevin Irvin
Phoenix, AZ

Thought and Memory Table 2000
Ebonized and bleached maple, italia wood, bronze
37"h × 19"w × 15"d

After having sculpted for several years, I became intrigued by the challenge of making functional pieces— furniture that would incorporate aspects of sculpture, both in its aesthetic approach and, literally, in the use of small bronze sculpture as functional elements. I begin by fashioning bronze castings that will serve as a piece's drawer pulls before proceeding to design the actual furniture that will act as their "frame." Architectural references are a constant in my work. I enjoy the challenge of combining styles like classical Roman, Asian, and contemporary architecture in a single piece.

Photo: William McKellar

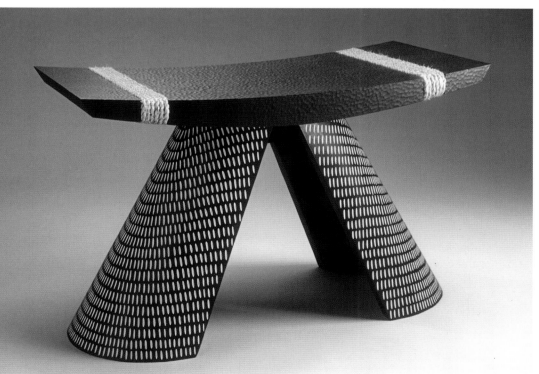

Douglas Finkel
Richmond, VA

Source Bench 1999, from an edition of 30 in production since 1998
Poplar, rope, paint
16"h × 27"w × 12"d

The design for this bench is inspired by African headrests and Samurai headdresses. It is one of a series that uses the same form and explores a variety of textures, colors, and materials. Collection: Renwick Gallery, Smithsonian Institution.

Photo: Double Image Studios

Richard Judd
Belleville, WI

Carved Mahogany Bench 1999
Mahogany
18"h × 60"w × 18"d

*Inspired by the beautiful plank of
mahogany. Each leg is made up of four
pieces of mahogany. I tried to overbuild
the joint, as there would be
considerable leverage. There are two
large tenons and two threaded inserts
and threaded rods on each end.*

Photo: Bill Lemke

Andy Buck
Rochester, NY

Listeners 2000
Mahogany, milk paint
36"h × 16"w × 17"d

Conversation chairs.

Photo: Geoff Tesch

Brent Skidmore
Charlotte, NC

Egg Boulders with Vanity Plane 2000

Basswood, mirror, acrylic paint
75"h × 18"w × 14"d

*I make a fair number of mirrors that usually
hang on the wall. This piece is the first to
stand on the floor. I plan to use my attraction
to rock cairns as a starting point in the earlier
ones and see where this new series goes.*

Photo: David Ramsey

Miguel Gomez-Ibañez
Weston, MA

High Chest of Drawers
1999

Cherry case, madrone
burl, carpathian elm burl,
banding of bloodwood
and purpleheart
68" h × 38" w × 21" d

*The form of this chest is
based on designs from the
William and Mary period.
The surface decoration is not
traditional in that it does not
follow the outlines of the
drawers. It reminds me of
the geometric borders of
Amish quilts from the 1800s
or the geometric studies of
abstract art a century later.
The pattern becomes more
elaborate as it rises to
support a deep cornice, and
its design is based on Louis
Sullivan's ideas about the
early Chicago skyscrapers.
Surely the William and Mary
high chest was the skyscraper
of its time. In both cases
the designers developed
an articulated, rustic base;
a plain, repetitive middle
section; smaller and more
numerous openings toward
the top; and a rich
overhanging cornice.*

Photo: Dean Powell

Derek Secor Davis
Boulder, CO

Broken Sphere Bench 2000
Cherry, poplar, milk paint, concrete
32"h × 72"w × 21"d

*This piece is a composite of the organic and industrial
elements found in the human experience. It is a statement
on the often uncomfortable balance between the two.*

Photo: John Bonath, Maddog Studio

Understanding Tradition

MIGUEL GOMEZ-IBAÑEZ

Not a style or a category, tradition is the medium that connects
furniture makers to each other and to the rest of the world

It is unfortunate that traditional furniture makers and contemporary furniture makers are often seen in different camps. It's a distinction that, at its most polarized, characterizes one group as involved in irrelevant period reproductions, while the other group creates something that's, well, not really furniture. For some, judgmental overtones stem from modern notions of art and artists that put a premium on innovation and originality. For others, the judgments favor familiarity, continuity, and conservatism.

But this distinction ignores the ties that connect makers, whatever their inclinations. To appreciate these ties will require makers of "art furniture" to see themselves more clearly as working within a tradition, and the makers of "period furniture" to see themselves more accurately as interpreters of our society, expressing contemporary culture and values. All furniture makers are, in some sense, traditional. The work of two current furniture makers illustrates this point.

Harold Ionson, 80, is a Massachusetts furniture maker who has spent the past thirteen years creating nine replicas of the historic "Derby" commode, made in 1809 by Thomas Seymour and a centerpiece of the collection of American furniture at the Museum of Fine Arts, Boston. At the meeting of the newly formed Society of American Period Furniture Makers at Colonial Williamsburg in 1999, Ionson received the first annual Cartouche Award for lifetime achievement, given in recognition of his work over the past forty years creating meticulously crafted reproductions of a number of antique furniture forms.

In contrast, Philadelphia furniture maker Peter Handler has spent the past eighteen years designing and making hundreds of pieces of original furniture for a long list of clients. College educated and with advanced degrees in the visual arts, he creates chairs and tables of anodized aluminum, glass, granite, laminate, and fabric in vibrant colors and curving, free-form shapes, giving them names like "Giraffe," "Calamari," and "Praying Mantis." His work (see page 112) was selected by the Smithsonian Institution for inclusion in the Smithsonian Craft Show 2000, a juried exhibition of artists whose work, according to its own promotion, exemplifies "a pursuit of original ideas and a strong sense of personal expression."

Most people would identify Ionson as a traditional furniture maker, and Handler as a contemporary furniture maker. Such a characterization would be both superficial and inaccurate.

Peter Handler spends his days in a small workshop in northwest Philadelphia, assisted by an apprentice who is the latest of many young people employed and trained in his shop, a number of whom have gone on to start their own furniture-making businesses. His furniture, designed in a contemporary style, is made to order, generally on commission from upper-income clients eager to own a piece that reflects their taste and accomplishments, one that has the resonance of a traditional, expertly crafted, hand-made object.

Harold Ionson, on the other hand, is not a furniture maker by profession. "You can't make any money building furniture," he says. Although Ionson trained during his high school years as a cabinetmaker, he worked for nearly forty years as a union carpenter building custom forms for concrete structures and turned to furniture making only when he retired. He now works alone in the garage behind his home in suburban Boston. In this setting, and because he does not depend on making furniture to produce an income, Ionson's involvement in furniture making is more typical of a modern hobbyist than of a traditional cabinetmaker, his considerable skills notwithstanding.

Both Handler and Ionson rely on machines to produce their furniture, but Handler is quick to point out that cabinetmakers have always relied upon lathes and any other power tools that were available. While he is immersed in current metal-working technology, Handler wants to remain first and foremost a designer who works closely and personally with his clients. "Technology is not a source of inspiration," he says, "it's just a tool. The center of each design is the client."

Ionson's production techniques also rely heavily on modern machine tools, which are particularly useful because he is building the commodes as a limited production run of nine. "I prefer multiples," says Ionson. He loves designing and building the jigs and fixtures, which, in combination with his power tools, make construction more efficient. But despite the economic advantages of Ionson's limited-production run, his commodes are being sold through an art gallery, at a price near $130,000 each.

Although it is obvious that Ionson's commodes represent nineteenth-century tastes, and Handler's designs represent more contemporary sensibilities, it's perhaps not so obvious that Ionson is typical of many contemporary furniture makers, while Handler is more like a traditional one.

While Handler makes his living working in a small shop with apprentices, as did Philadelphia furniture makers of the nineteenth century, Ionson, of independent means, works at home by himself. While Handler designs and sells individual commissioned pieces directly to his clients, as furniture makers have traditionally done, Ionson sells his furniture in an art gallery; a distinctly modern innovation. Ionson may be creating replicas of Thomas Seymour's work, but it is Handler who is carrying the furniture-making tradition represented by Seymour's shop into the twenty-first century.

Traditional, Contemporary, and Progressive Relationships

As this comparison indicates, the labels of "traditional" furniture maker and "contemporary" furniture maker can be misleading. In fact tradition is integral to the work of both Ionson and Handler, as it is to the work of all furniture makers.

Traditional or contemporary? Harold Ionson's Derby commodes look traditional, while Peter Handler's aluminum-frame chairs look contemporary. But like most fine artists, Ionson works alone and markets through art galleries, whereas Handler works with a small team of helpers and apprentices and, like furniture makers of yore, deals directly with his clients.

Sam Maloof's signature rocker combines traditional, contemporary, and progressive ideas.

The carved seat and curved back with shaped splats reflect Maloof's sensitivity toward ergonomics, a progressive idea for the time (the 1950s) when Maloof began developing these chairs.

Transitional Work

Looking backward, the idea that traditional, contemporary, and progressive elements co-exist in a single piece of furniture runs counter to the popular conception of the history of furniture as a succession of styles in chronological order. This view of furniture history as a linear progression papers over the muddled way in which some styles come and go and then come back again, while other styles, like colonial furniture, never seem to disappear.

In the seventeenth and eighteenth centuries, for example, we are taught that the William and Mary (Mannerist) style was replaced by the Queen Anne (Baroque) style, which in turn was replaced by Chippendale (Rococo), which finally was eclipsed by the Federal (Neo-Classical) style.

This concept of tradition as something common to all makers is presented by Henry Glassie in his essay "Folk Art," which describes the relationship between the ideas behind a maker's work and the culture in which he or she works.[1] According to Glassie, some ideas are conservative, some are normative, and some are progressive. Glassie's terms might be paraphrased as traditional, contemporary, and avant garde. If a maker's idea is old within the maker's own culture, that idea is conservative, or traditional. If an idea is representative of the maker's culture, it is normative or contemporary. Avant garde or progressive ideas are ahead of their time.

Glassie explains, "These abstract distinctions are most useful when thought of as opposing forces having simultaneous existence in the mind of every individual, though one or another of the modes of thinking may predominate in certain individuals or in the groups they combine to form." Glassie observes that elements of traditionalism, popular culture, and progressivism coexist not only in the mind of a maker but also simultaneously in the maker's work.

This amalgam of traditional, contemporary, and progressive design ideas within a single object certainly characterizes studio furniture today. It can be seen in the work of Sam Maloof, whose rocking chairs draw on familiar images of traditional porch rockers and Windsor chairs. Shaping the joints to create flowing, curvilinear forms, Maloof reminds us that the chair is sculpture as well as functional object, a contemporary notion.

1. For Glassie's essay and others that explore this subject, see Richard Dorson, ed., *Folklore and Folklife* (Chicago: University of Chicago Press, 1972).

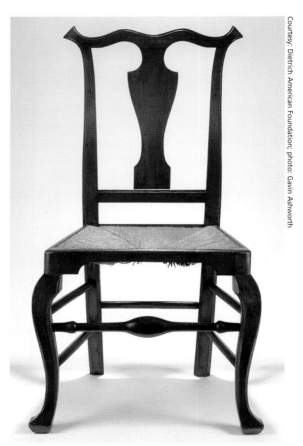

Styles change gradually. This transitional chair, made in Philadelphia around 1750, combines the then new Rococo crest rail with then current Queen Anne back splat and legs, atop a rustic rush seat and stretcher turnings held over from the era of William and Mary.

While stylistic labels can help clarify and describe, they oversimplify the complex evolutionary nature of furniture history. In America during the seventeenth and eighteenth centuries new designs were introduced gradually, with some elements changed and some maintained, as furniture makers tentatively explored new ideas while continuing to make the older styles.

"Change was most often gradual," writes Jack L. Lindsey in the catalog for "Worldly Goods," the Philadelphia Museum of Art's 1999 exhibition on the arts of early Pennsylvania, "with decorative elements of a new style cautiously applied to earlier forms, requiring no abrupt shift in mind set, for transitional experiments toward a new mode of decoration or a new form could continue to carry the symbolic significance of older styles."[2]

There are many examples of transitional pieces of furniture that include elements of more than one labeled style. Lindsey illustrates his point with a chair made in Philadelphia around 1750 when the Chippendale style was beginning to take hold. The new Rococo design motifs can be seen in the crest rail, with its ogee curves and prominent ears. But below the crest rail this chair is an eclectic mix: a Queen Anne vase-shaped splat and cabriole legs, a rush seat and a bulbous turned front stretcher. The seat and stretcher are typical of the William and Mary style, by then supposedly out of date for more than fifty years and, even in 1750, clearly "traditional."

Such transitional pieces have often been described as the work of unsophisticated craftsmen working in a rural setting. But a furniture maker who had the skills and knowledge of design to create either a carved Chippendale crest rail or a characteristic Queen Anne splat clearly could have carried through in either style. But he or she didn't, choosing instead a compromise that spans several generations of style.

Lindsey explains that furniture makers in the seventeenth and eighteenth centuries relied upon historical or traditional design elements in their work to provide a sense of reassurance and continuity in what was essentially a conservative market. The same can be said of furniture makers today, including Sam Maloof, who uses traditional design motifs to add a reassuring resonance to his contemporary designs.

2. Jack L. Lindsey, *Worldly Goods, The Arts of Early Pennsylvania 1688–1758* (Philadelphia: Philadelphia Museum of Art, 1999), p. 7.

The Dunlap brothers, working in New Hampshire at the end of the eighteenth century, made traditional Scots-Irish furniture, such as this side chair (1770–1792), for an immigrant clientele who found comfort in its familiar vocabulary.

Expressing Cultural Values

Another motivation for re-using traditional or historical forms has been to express the particular culture of the maker or the marketplace. The distinctive furniture of the Dunlap brothers, who worked in southern New Hampshire at the end of the eighteenth century, was thought for years to represent the unique designs of a talented but idiosyncratic furniture family. Furniture historian Philip Zea has demonstrated that in fact their furniture is directly related to design elements found in Scots-Irish wainscot chairs of the previous century.[3] The Dunlap brothers were indeed talented designers and craftsmen, but their furniture expresses both their own cultural heritage and the Scots-Irish cultural heritage of their community.

The work of Virginia cabinetmaker Johannes Spitler and other ethnic craftsmen working in post-Revolutionary America should also be seen in this light. Spitler's chests incorporate design elements taken from previous generations of Swiss-German cabinetmakers, re-used to express a cultural heritage shared with many of his Virginia

3. See Philip Zea and Donald Dunlap, *The Dunlap Cabinetmakers, A Tradition in Craftsmanship* (Mechanicsburg, PA: Stackpole Books, 1994) and David Learmont, "The Trinity Hall Chairs, Aberdeen" in *Furniture History, Vol. 14* (1978), pp. 1–8.

Johannnes Spitler's painted chests proudly declared his Swiss-German origins in the melting pot of post-Revolutionary America (above, 1795–1807). The contemporary artist Cheryl Riley draws from her own heritage, as well as from other cultures she admires (far right, "Luba Yoruba Chest," 1994). Harold Rittenberry expresses the rural South with found materials (right, "Southern Charm Fan," 1998). He exemplifies the bricoleur, the eloquent craftsman-of-opportunity found in every culture worldwide.

neighbors, and presumably to give his customers a reassuring sense of community and belonging.[4]

Today such expressions of ethnic and cultural heritage can be seen in the work of Cheryl Riley, whose furniture designs draw upon images and motifs taken from previous generations of African-American artists as well as from other cultures that have inspired her.

The expression of a cultural tradition can also be seen in materials and methods of work rather than in the forms of the furniture. Harold Rittenberry, a contemporary African-American furniture

maker from Georgia, sees himself as working within a rural Southern tradition that is neither black nor white. "In the South people were poor," says Rittenberry, "and that's why you have people making furniture. If you saw something in a store and you couldn't afford to buy it, you went out to the barn and you just started making it. Black or white, if you needed a piece of furniture, you came home after work and you made one." Rittenberry bought a welder in 1985 and started making furniture out of scrap metal. His "Southern Charm Fan" settee, made of old gears, bent wire, and tubular steel, is of no identifiable style. Blending images of fans, carpet beaters, and wrought iron railings, it expresses, above all, a tradition of making do with the materials at hand.

Making a Statement

Whether furniture uses an earlier generation's forms to express a cultural heritage or, as previously demonstrated, to satisfy a conservative marketplace, the effect is the same. Old and recognizable design elements provide a sense of reassurance and continuity. But there are more provocative motivations for re-using traditional or

4. For more on the work of Spitler see Ronald L. Hurst and Jonathan Prown, *Southern Furniture 1680–1830, The Colonial Williamsburg Collection* (New York, Harry N. Abrams, 1997).

historical forms. They can also express a political or philosophical statement, as was the case in America at the end of the eighteenth century.

By the 1790s, America had emerged from the difficult economic times that followed the Revolution and was beginning to experience growing power and influence. Economic prosperity fueled a desire for a new style of furniture as well, one that would reflect the ideals and ambitions of the new democracy. Furniture designers, inspired by the recent excavations of Herculaneum and Pompeii, turned to ancient Greece and Rome, civilization's first democracies, as fitting models for the new Federal style.

One characteristic example of the new style is the klismos chair, with its saber legs and sweeping curves of the back and crest rail. The origin of this form can be found in images from Greek vases and sculpture, images that were appropriated by the new republic to evoke past democratic ideals. In the hands of American craftsmen and designers, however, the Greek and Roman images acquired elaborate stenciled, carved, and gilded ornamental details, creating new forms evocative of ancient culture that appealed to the aspirations of wealthy merchants from Boston to Baltimore.

Colonial Revival and the Arts and Crafts Movement are two later examples of furniture makers turning to the designs of a previous era to make political statements. The earlier of the two, Colonial Revival, has proved to be the most enduring. The beginnings of Colonial Revival can be traced back to 1840 and the presidential campaign of William Henry Harrison. He campaigned on a theme of a return to the simple values and self-reliance of Colonial America. To make his point, he had log cabins erected around the country, including one in Providence, Rhode Island, that were furnished with examples of colonial furniture and decorative arts.[5]

The use of images of colonial furniture to recall an idealized America continued through the Centennial celebrations of 1876 and into the beginning of the twentieth century, most notably through the efforts of Wallace Nutting. In 1917, after years of collecting and documenting colonial furniture, Nutting began to produce hand-

Courtesy: Winterthur Museum

With imagery from ancient Greece and Rome, this Federal armchair (left, circa 1825) manifests the national ideals of the young republic. The simple yet energetic turnings of Jon Siegel's gateleg table (below, 1997) recall the foundational values and self-reliance of Colonial America.

Dean Powell

made versions of his favorite designs. Colonial Revival was particularly popular during the Depression era of the 1930s, when Americans needed a great deal of reassurance. It was during the 1930s that Colonial Williamsburg began its own program of furniture reproduction, and it continues today. Among contemporary studio furniture makers Jon Siegel's work stands out for its connection with and advancement of Wallace Nutting's powerful Colonial Revival legacy.

Both commercial and studio furniture makers today commonly rely on historic images to make a political statement or provide a philosophical basis for their work. Shaker style permeates con-

5. For the origins of Colonial Revival in the Harrison campaign see Christopher P. Monkhouse and Thomas S. Michie, *American Furniture in Pendleton House* (Providence: The Rhode Island School of Design, 1986).

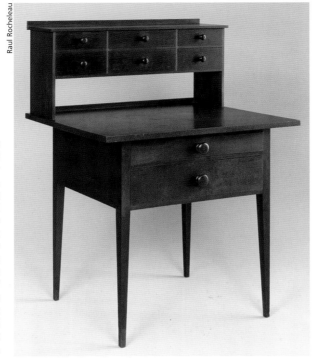

Raul Rocheleau

The Shaker craftsmen of the nineteenth century found peace in the rhythms of their work. Eschewing ostentation, they put their hands to the rightful use of materials, and their eyes to godly proportions (right, work stand, 1874). Contemporary artist James Krenov achieves composure in his furniture by immersing himself wholeheartedly in the craftsman's timeless quest for harmony of body and mind (below, cabinet on stand, 1996).

David Welter

temporary furniture making to such an extent that it is no longer seen as a historic style, but rather a contemporary one. The impact of the simple, straightforwardly joined, undecorated furniture produced in Shaker communities in the mid 1800s is now seen everywhere, from Crate and Barrel to the elegant lines and sensitive detailing of furniture maker James Krenov.

Krenov, in his most recent book *With Wakened Hands*, sounds a distinctively Shaker theme when he writes: "In these times of ever increasing self-assertion when people seek the new, the garish and the striking, the craftsman's timeless quest is nearly forgotten." One hundred years earlier, Shaker cabinetmaker Orren Haskins (1815–1892) made a similar observation in his diary: "The world at large can scarcely keep pace with itself in its styles and fashions which last but a short time, when something still more worthless or absurd takes its place."

Haskins devoted his life to a spiritual path expressed in his cabinetmaking. He regarded his work as a meditation. Similarly, Krenov writes of his devotion to "making a living by making fine things and through the making, finding happiness…. Most of the ease and enjoyment of woodworking comes through the simple processes that require harmony, both mentally and physically."[6]

Associationalism

Shaker style represents cultural values of simplicity, honesty, and spirituality, just as Colonial Revival furniture reaffirmed the values of individuality and self-reliance, and Federal furniture embodied the democratic ideals of the new nation. In each case, there is an understanding that furniture has the power to convey symbolic meaning. That power has been termed "associationalism" by art historian George L. Hersey.

Humans, according to the theory of associationalism described by Hersey, are endowed with the power of imagination, or the ability to make associations. Objects, on the other hand, possess an expressive power, or a power to evoke associations. The role of education, according to Hersey, is to "equip our minds with as many asso-

6. To compare Haskins and Krenov see Erin M. Burdis, *Making His Mark: The Work of Shaker Craftsman Orren Haskins* (Old Chatham, NY: Shaker Museum and Library, 1997, and James Krenov, *With Wakened Hands: Furniture by James Krenov and Students* (Bethel, CT: Cambium Press, 2000).

ciations as possible, or to develop imagination." The role of the artist is to make objects as expressive as possible.[7]

Hersey's theory is helpful in understanding the furniture of Tommy Simpson, among other contemporary furniture makers. Simpson's "Boston Throne Chair," produced in 1989 for the New American Furniture exhibit in Boston, and the many chairs that have followed (including one pictured on page 93) use carving, paint, and other objects applied to the form of a traditional Windsor chair to provoke thoughts, reactions, reflections, and laughter.

But while Hersey's writings on associationalism seem to describe perfectly the work of contemporary studio furniture makers like Simpson, Hersey was referring to designers in nineteenth-century Victorian England who, in their writings on eclecticism, sought to justify their re-use of historical forms in art and architecture on a theoretical or philosophical basis.

Some of the furniture produced during this time, such as the Gothic Revival furniture of A. W.N. Pugin (1812–1852), was intended to evoke notions of aristocratic chivalry and the cultural distinctiveness of England. The elements of Classical, Japanese, and ancient Egyptian furniture employed by E.W. Godwin (1833–1886) and others recalled Britain's past glories and "the ethos of nation and Empire."[8]

Godwin and Pugin, like Simpson, Krenov, and Haskins, have employed traditional or historical forms for the same reasons that countless other furniture makers have: artistic expression and marketability. These motivations have not changed significantly for hundreds of years.

Breaking with the Past

But if the re-use of historic forms and images is as prevalent today as it was in the past, why do many furniture makers who use recognizably traditional forms feel that they have no place in the world of contemporary studio furniture? It may be a legacy of the Modern movement that started

Courtesy V&A Picture Library

in Europe in the beginning of the twentieth century, which was characterized by the belief that past forms of expression were not only irrelevant to a modern world, they acted as constraints, preventing designers from achieving the goal of a truly contemporary style. The influential architect and furniture designer Le Corbusier proclaimed that "past decisions, customs, habits, all these stay with us...disturbing, constricting, wantonly interfering with the free play of the mind."[9]

Le Corbusier, with Walter Gropius, Mies van der Rohe, and other Modernist designers who emerged after the upheaval of World War I, set out to develop a new design vocabulary for both architecture and the decorative arts. They found inspiration in locomotives, steamships, airplanes, and other contemporary forms with little or no historical precedent. Le Corbusier wrote in 1923 that a designer "will find in a steamship his freedom from age-long but contemptible enslavement to the past."[10] At the same time Gropius established the Bauhaus in Germany, a design school

The eclectic E.W. Godwin expressed the glory of the British Empire by pillaging forms and images from cultures it had overrun as well as from previous empires (sideboard, 1867).

---

7. For the philosophical basis of late nineteenth century eclecticism see George L. Hersey, *High Victorian Gothic: A Study in Associationalism* (Baltimore, MD: The Johns Hopkins University Press, 1972).

8. Susan Weber Soros, *The Secular Furniture of E.W. Godwin* (New York: The Bard Graduate Center and Yale University Press, 1999).

9. Charles Edouard Jenneret, Le Corbusier, *The Modulor*, a translation of the 1954 text (Cambridge, MA: MIT Press, 1968), p. 242.

10. From Le Corbusier's *Vers Une Architecture*, as quoted in Reyner Banham, *Theory and Design in the First Machine Age* (London: The Architectural Press, 1960).

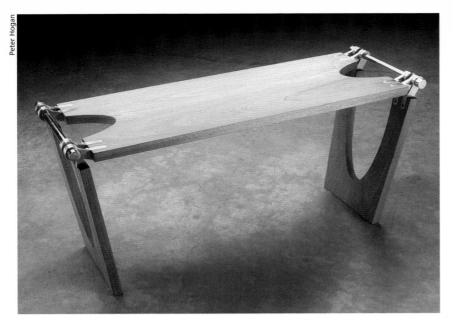

Modernism today. Scott Currie's folding table ("Transient," 2000), which comes with a canvas carrying case, expresses the Modernist values of innovation and unity in function and form.

where the teachers, according to instructor Josef Albers, "did not look back…but intentionally opposed what had already been done and said."[11] With Modernism came a new morality, and the belief that imitation was not honorable or worthy. Authenticity, innovation, and newness became the primary values. Today Modernism itself has become a historical movement, but its fundamental drive for originality and reinvention can still be seen in the work of many contemporary studio furniture makers, such as Scott Currie of Stoney Creek, Ontario, who focus on innovations in function, structure, and form.

The Modernist designers in the first half of the twentieth century believed they should develop a new aesthetic that was suited to the industrial and technological realities in which they lived and worked. Their goal of developing a style of furniture design appropriate for its time was not new or remarkable. What was remarkable was the belief that it could be achieved only by breaking from all aspects of the past.

For centuries furniture designers have struggled to find a style or form of expression appropriate for the times in which they lived. With the exception of the relatively short-lived period of Modernism, that search always included an examination of the past. This was the case with Godwin and Pugin, and it was true a century before that, when Thomas Chippendale (1715–1762) published *The Gentleman and Cabinetmaker's Director.*

Chippendale's designs included chairs, tables, and bookcases embellished with the pointed arches and trefoils found in the English churches of the Middle Ages, which he thought created a particularly English furniture style appropriate for his times. But Chippendale's Gothic designs were not copies of Gothic furniture. They were contemporary interpretations of that style, and as such reflected the period in which they were produced, just as Gothic and Federal furniture a century later reflected the aspirations and sensibilities of nineteenth century society.

"It is easy enough to make up furniture in direct imitation of any particular style," wrote Godwin in 1874. "What I have endeavored to secure in design has rather been a modern treatment of certain well-known and admired styles."[12] Echoing Godwin, contemporary furniture historian Gerald Ward writes in *The Eye of the Beholder,* "A revival implies a rebirth and subsequent growth. It is no mere copying or reproducing of an age past, rather it is a dynamic reinterpretation of that age in terms of the present."[13]

Even contemporary furniture makers who create furniture that many would describe as reproductions are not simply recreating the past. First, with rare exceptions, the materials and methods used by furniture makers like Harold Ionson are not those used in 1809. Even if they were, as is the case with a small group of reproduction furniture makers, a highboy or secretary produced by hand today is not comparable in our society to one produced in the society of three centuries ago. Today it is built as either a museum piece or a statement in support of a sense of lost art and craftsmanship.

The best furniture makers of every age are able to absorb and synthesize a pre-existing form into a new artistic statement capable of standing on its own merits. They take liberties with the original object that is their inspiration, adapting it to a more contemporary function, production method or, more subtly, sense of design or "taste."

The Shape of Time

The idea that "revival," "traditional," or even "reproduction" furniture is not in fact a copy but

---

11. For the recollections of Josef Albers and other Bauhaus participants, see Eckhard Neuman, ed., *Bauhaus and Bauhaus People* (New York: Van Nostrand Reinhold, 1970).

12. Soros, op. cit., p. 25.

13. Ward goes on to argue that objects unavoidably reflect the times in which they are produced in *The Eye of the Beholder: Fakes, Replicas and Alterations in American Art* (New Haven: Yale University Press, 1977).

a contemporary adaptation of the past brings us back to Henry Glassie's initial point. Traditional influences or ideas coexist and compete with contemporary and progressive ideas, not only in the minds of the makers but also in the objects.

George Kubler in *The Shape of Time,* an analysis of the history of art, goes further, arguing that repetition (tradition) and innovation are inextricably linked—nor would we want it any other way. Innovation is not possible without tradition, because tradition is the context for the departure, and without context the departure cannot be understood. Repetition alone would be intolerably boring. On the other hand, endless invention would be chaos. We require a combination of repetition and innovation.[14]

Tradition, argue Kubler and Glassie, is present in every action. It can be employed consciously or unconsciously, overtly or subtly, but it is nevertheless found in the ideas of all makers and in all the objects they produce. This sense of tradition is also directly linked to our ability to relate to an object, to respond to it, and ultimately to place a value on it.

According to this argument, if we respond to a piece of furniture, it is because we recognize something familiar in it. The sense of recognition implies the recurrence of something from the past. Recognition requires repetition. In a related way, when we make value judgments, those judgments occur within a frame of reference, which must necessarily be anchored in the past.

The past itself attracts us, according to Kubler. "The retention of old things," he writes, "has always been a central ritual in human societies. Its contemporary expression in the public museums of the world rises from extremely deep roots…going back to the royal collections and the cathedral treasuries of earlier ages."

Beyond the generalized human drive to preserve the past, Kubler finds a related desire to set all things within the context of the past, or to set each object within a recognizable series. He sees this quality as critical for the valuation of a work of art:

> A pleasure shared by artists, collectors and historians alike is the discovery that an old and interesting work of art is not unique, but that its type exists in a variety of examples spread early and late in time, as well as high and low upon a scale of quality, in versions which are antetypes and derivatives, originals and copies, transformations and variants. Much of our satisfaction in these circumstances arises from the contemplation of a formal sequence, from an intuitive sense of enlargement and completion in the presence of a shape in time.

This process, which Kubler calls "serial appreciation," informs the concepts of connoisseurship and provenance in furniture. An object is set for comparison within a larger group of objects that are similar in style or in the details of craftsmanship or in their history. It is the appreciation of the differences between objects that is the key to the evaluation (and thus the valuation) of each.

All of this suggests that furniture which relates to a past context, which incorporates or refers to known objects, or which is able to be placed within a series of similar objects, will be by its nature more valuable than an object with no recognizable relationship to the past.[15] The Beanbag chair might serve as an example to prove this point. Designed in 1968 and included in the exhibit and book *100 Masterpieces from the Vitra Design Museum Collection,* the Beanbag chair attempted a complete break from the past. But it remains today an isolated object, unrelated to either any previous furniture form or any tradition in craftsmanship. It is valued by the Vitra Design Museum as an idea, but society as a whole does not value it as furniture.

It is difficult to find examples like the Beanbag chair that are devoid of references to the past. This is because the past is nearly inescapable. The past, or tradition in this sense, defines the context in which all furniture makers work, whether consciously or unconsciously. Further, it defines the context of everyone who buys and appreciates furniture. Thus tradition is not a style or category but the medium that connects furniture makers to each other and to the rest of the world. Tradition isn't about "us versus them"—it's just about us. ■

Uncomfortable, unattractive, and short-lived in the marketplace, the "Beanbag Chair" (designed by Piero Gatti, Cesare Paolini, and Franco Teodoro in 1968) nevertheless was a new expression in furniture design. It illustrates just how difficult it is to make a complete break with our furniture heritage.

Courtesy: Vitra Design Museum

14. The following quotations are taken from George Kubler, *The Shape of Time* (New Haven: Yale University Press, 1973), pp. 80 and 45.

15. Alexander von Vegesack, *100 Masterpieces from the Vitra Design Museum Collection* (Weil am Rhein: Germany, The Vitra Design Museum, 1996).

More Beauty and More Deep Wonder

MARK KINGWELL

Tables, chairs, and other machines for thinking

It's a curious fact, but one not often remarked, that philosophers have no sense of furniture. Curious because, after all, they spend at least as much time sitting and lying and lounging as the rest of the populace—maybe more so when it comes to lying and lounging, actually. And yet in the vast volumes of Plato and Aristotle, of Kant and Hume, you will not find, to my knowledge, any serious consideration of what they are sitting, lying, or lounging on.

There are many thousands of pages on the nature of knowledge, the question of the meaning of Being, and how to live an examined life. There is scarcely a line on how to know, make, or examine a table or a chair. What of sofas, for example? How many philosophers have wondered about a couch the way they have wondered about relations of logical entailment? You might think this is to be expected, if not quite forgivable. Philosophers have also largely ignored food, sex, personal grooming, and the common cold. Most of them think, and many of them say, that they have more important things to deal with. There is, as a result, no philosophy of furniture.

Of course there are a few prominent exceptions, though they tend to be among the most amateur of the philosophical ranks, the not-quite-serious members of the tribe whose reputations depend on other achievements and interests. This is not coincidental, for genuine attention leads, perhaps necessarily, to a decidedly unprofessional undermining of the philosophical profession's peculiar form of blinkered self-regard. Jean-Paul Sartre, for example, established himself as a free-ranging intellectual, not a professional philosopher in the academic sense. He made it his mission to speak to the deepest of human concerns, and his works have suffered a regrettable decline in academic reputation as a result. Sartre makes a point of letting us know that the immovable furnishings of existential hell, in the play *Huis Clos,* was of tasteless Second Empire design, as if to underscore the fact that eternal misery is more often banal and tacky than fascinatingly inventive. And if we consider Freud a philosopher (either a dangerous or an obvious proposition, depending on the company), he is exceptional in fixating on a couch—one which was, as we know, rather unremarkable in dimensions and covered with a layer of Turkish rugs.

In Plato's *Republic,* Socrates (another principled amateur) introduces the famous figure of a bed to illustrate the theory of the Forms: those timeless essences wherein genuine truth resides. A painting of a bed, he notes, is merely a reflection of an actual bed fashioned by a craftsman. But this three-dimensional bed is itself just as much a reflection, a pale copy, of the ideal bed, the Form of the bed, bedness itself. Each reflection—Form of bed, actual bed, picture of bed, reflection of picture of bed, and so on—represents a declension from Reality, a loss of metaphysical firmness. You can lie on only one of these beds, in short, as Socrates famously does while talking of love in the *Symposium,* but for Plato (here using Socrates as his mouthpiece) the truly real bed is precisely the one you can't lie on, namely the ideal form of bed, or what we might call Bed. And while Bed may be metaphysically interesting, indeed fascinating, it is not what you or I would consider a good option when it comes to supporting the futon or Sealy Posturpedic. However

Illustrations by Gerrit Gollner

higher up the ladder of reality than physical beds it may be, Plato's Bed will not hold you up when you simply need to lie down.

Socrates sometimes lounged on a couch as well, because the Greek word for bed can also mean couch. The piece of furniture in question in the *Symposium* was used for both conversation and sleep—not to mention seduction, as when Alcibiades, in an ancient preview of the modern teenage mating ritual, attempted to put the moves on Socrates when the night grew late and the light grew low. Mostly, however, Socrates prowled the Athenian marketplace on foot to pursue his thoughts about justice and virtue. Indeed, philosophers seem to agree with Aristotle, founder of what is actually known as the Peripatetic School, that thinking is something best done while walking.

The philosopher in Iris Murdoch's novel *The Philosopher's Pupil* cannot think unless he is strolling and in conversation, and Nietzsche famously said, "Only thoughts that come from walking have any value." And yet, no walking thought is anything more than half-formed, and he had to sit down somewhere long enough to write that. It is worth remembering that we would not have the benefit of Nietzsche's, or anyone else's, wisdom were it not for the chairs they sat in and the tables they wrote upon. Ludwig Wittgenstein notoriously placed himself in a canvas deck chair every day in his rooms in King's College, Cambridge, there to think the thoughts that might, on a good day, make it into one of his notebooks. More often, he sat and thought and wrote nothing, or rose the next morning to crumple what he had written the day before. My point is this: Wittgenstein should have spared some of those thoughts for the deck chair itself. And that point leads to an even larger claim: despite centuries of effort to make philosophy dead from the neck down, we are still embodied creatures with limbs and frames requiring support.

The Role That Furniture Plays

The question of furniture is thus, in its way, a question about the site of reflection, the scene where thinking happens. Given the importance of time spent in the study, it is therefore remarkable how little of reflection's attention is directed towards its own conditions of possibility. To be sure, there are once more oddball exceptions.

Kierkegaard spends a good deal of time, some would say too much, considering the nature of his writing table. Among other things, Kierkegaard underwrites a certain romantic interest in the particular table or desk where a work was composed, an interest that is widely accepted but not often investigated critically. Here one might think, for example, of the 1996 collection of photographs by Jill Krementz called *The Writers' Desk,* depicting various twentieth-century authors in their scenes of writing: Joyce Carol Oates's tiny shelf, Saul Bellow's modified altar-contraption. The auratic associations of Dickens' desk or Tennessee Williams' sawhorse desk or Pablo Neruda's bureaucratic Cadillac of a desk—the particular ink stains and carved-in words of the article of furniture—may thus point us toward what makes furniture worthy of philosophical consideration.

But ultimately those associations blind us, as auras so often do, to the deeper issue of how the mundane and the profound are related. How, precisely, does a particular article of furniture accommodate certain thoughts and not others? Would Kierkegaard have written differently if he had a smaller table? What has the proliferation of the laptop done to the act of thinking, especially as transformed into prose? The novelist Richard Ford has said he can write anywhere, in a crowded room or airport departure lounge; Raymond Carver allegedly preferred his stationary car for an office. Does that matter to the question of how deeply Ford or Carver (or anyone) can think? For thinking is, after all, the present concern. Interest in the writer's desk focuses more often on writers of fiction than of non-fiction, especially of philosophy—as if the rarefied thoughts of philosophy were necessarily less embodied than the muddy labors of fiction. This, once more, works paradoxically to squeeze the human life out of reflection as a mode, or act, of being human.

What is it to think? Where can it be done? Well or badly? Furniture takes its place in rooms, and the rooms where thought occurs are likewise

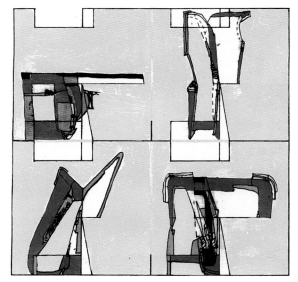

("I never read a book before reviewing it," he said; "it prejudices a man so"), once noted that there was "no furniture so charming as books." But, important as they are, books are not what we usually mean when we talk of furniture. Books that are merely furniture, perhaps purchased by the yard from remainder stock in order to outfit a pretentious bar or club, do not serve their purpose as books. Books are meant to be opened, one of these days anyway. In seeking a reflective philosophy of furniture we should rather focus on more basic items: tables, chairs, and other machines for thinking.

Lately, of course—especially in the last century and a half—there has been a vast new literature on the theory of design, including the design of furniture. Much of this literature is excellent, some of it is silly, and more than a little of it is incomprehensible. But in any event that is not what I mean by a philosophy of furniture. Design theory mostly involves extending principles of aesthetic evaluation from one realm, the fine arts, to another, the applied arts. It says little about the role that furniture plays in human life, little about the deepest first principles of what we might call the Furniture Idea.

I cannot hope to remedy the situation by myself. But I want to say a few words about what happens when we start thinking about tables and chairs as machines for thinking, essential supports for the essential human undertaking of reflection. This is, in its way, reflection on the act of reflection—and on the places where that reflection occurs. Furniture is a means to that end; it is also, as we shall see, an end in itself.

The Details Matter

There is, happily, an essay called "The Philosophy of Furniture." It was published in May of 1840 in a periodical called *Burton's Gentleman's Magazine*. But it is not by a philosopher, it is not really a philosophy, and it is not really about furniture.

When Edgar Allan Poe sat down (notably, we don't learn on or at what) to compose some thoughts on furniture, he was mainly interested in decorating taste, not the Furniture Idea. "The Philosophy of Furniture" begins by noting that different nations have different styles of decoration—the Spanish favoring drapes, but the French too distracted to decorate well, the Chinese too fanciful, and so on. "The Yankees alone

a subject worthy of more precise investigation. Montaigne, that most human of the great thinkers, a man willing to examine everything from table manners to his own sexual preferences and bodily functions, goes on at some length about his library and its furnishings. It was a circular room on the third floor of a tower standing at one corner of his property in southwestern France. It had three windows, a desk, a chair, and five tiers of shelves arranged in a semicircle. The shelves held Montaigne's collection of about a thousand books on philosophy, history, religion, and poetry.

"I spend most days of my life there, and most hours of each day," Montaigne wrote of the room, which had "splendid and unhampered views" and fifty-seven apposite quotations from his favorite authors painted on the wooden ceiling. Books are naturally the most important objects in a library, and as the novelist Anthony Powell said, they do furnish a room. The Rev. Sydney Smith, a man of great learning and wit are preposterous," he says, and proceeds to demolish the excesses of conspicuous consumption in a nation ruled more by money than taste.

"The cost of an article of furniture has at length come to be, with us, nearly the sole test of its merit in a decorative point of view," Poe complains, "and this test, once established, has led the way to many analogous errors, readily traceable to the one primitive folly." There is a basic confusion here of magnificence for beauty, argues Poe, and that leads Americans to what we can only describe today as stupid fashion mistakes. "Straight lines are too prevalent," he notes, "too uninterruptedly continued—or clumsily interrupted at right angles. If curved lines appear, they are repeated into unpleasant uniformity. By undue precision, the appearance of many a fine apartment is utterly spoiled."

As he goes on in this vein, Poe gradually acquires the definitive, slightly hysterical tones of a commentator on a home-and-garden television show. There is a lot of imperious talk about disastrous window treatments and unsuitable fabrics, many a harsh judgment of someone's bad endtables or ill-chosen color scheme. "The soul of the apartment is the carpet," Poe declares. "A judge at common law may be an ordinary man; a good judge of a carpet *must be* a genius. Yet we have heard discoursing of carpets...fellows who should not and who could not be entrusted with the management of their own *moustaches*." Turkish carpeting, he notes, is "taste in its dying agonies," while floral patterns "should not be endured within the limits of Christendom." We are forced to wonder: was Poe a frustrated interior designer?

Poe describes his own ideal apartment as a counterexample to all the excesses of glitter and mirrors and overdone drapes. Poe is explicit about the dreaminess of this room, its oneiric allure: "Even now, there is present to my mind's eye a small and not ostentatious chamber with whose decorations no fault can be found. The proprietor lies asleep upon a sofa....I will make a sketch of the room ere he awakes." By our standards it's still pretty over the top, but Poe's basic message of restraint is timeless:

> Two large low sofas of rosewood and crimson silk, gold-flowered, form the only seats, with the exception of two light conversation chairs, also of rose-wood. There is a pianoforte (rose-wood, also), without

cover, and thrown open. An octagonal table, formed altogether of the richest gold-threaded marble, is placed near one of the sofas. This is also without cover— the drapery of the curtains has been thought sufficient. Four large and gorgeous Sèvres vases, in which bloom a profusion of sweet and vivid flowers, occupy the slightly rounded angles of the room.... Some light and graceful hanging shelves, with golden edges and crimson silk cords with gold tassels, sustain two or three hundred magnificently bound books. Beyond these things, there is no furniture, if we except a Argand lamp, with a plain crimson-tinted ground-glass shade, which depends from the lofty vaulted ceiling by a single slender gold chain, and throws a tranquil but magical radiance over all.

By any standards, a good room. A room suitable for work but also for conversation, a place where a person might write a book or entertain a friend or carry on a love affair. In short, a place to think and dream and be human.

We may disagree with the details of Poe's taste—I would personally like to see a little less crimson and gold—but we cannot fault his intentions. Yet this is not really philosophy. There's something missing, namely consideration of *the very idea* of the chair or the table. The trouble on the other side is that philosophy seems to miss what Poe knows, namely that the details matter: that there's a difference between a Sèvres vase and something from Ikea; that rosewood is finer than pine; that too many mirrors spoil a room. Somewhere between *House Beautiful* and Plato's austere *Republic* lies the unexplored territory of a true philosophy of furniture. So far as the metaphysical illustration goes, Socrates' bed could just as easily be a boat or a horse.

Radical Doubt

When philosophers of the mainstream sort do write about furniture, in fact, they mostly do so as an act of annihilation. In his book *Meditations on First Philosophy,* for instance, Descartes mentions the study in which he is sitting, including the chair he uses to seat himself comfortably by the fire, and the table on which his writing materials lie. We might be forgiven for thinking that this laudable preoccupation with the conditions of thought is going to lead us to insight about the relation between furniture and reflec-

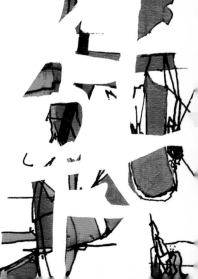

11

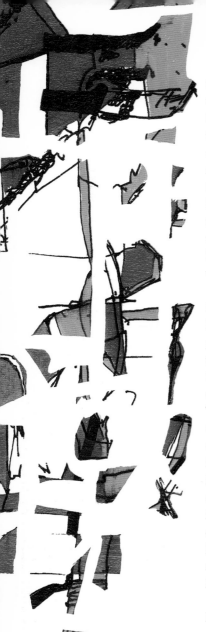

tion. But not really. Descartes is concerned only to give some sense of his immediate surroundings in order to add texture to his thinking—thinking which, indeed, involves immediately demolishing the very existence of those surroundings in a spasm of radical doubt. Descartes is interested in probing the evidence of his senses; he thinks we cannot know anything with certainty. So he starts with the handiest evidence, that of the stuff around him; and then proceeds, by bold steps, to show that he doesn't know what he thinks he knows.

That's how it mostly goes in philosophy, in fact, especially after Descartes: a lot of featureless furniture gets demolished in pursuit of the post-skeptical truth. The modern philosopher is taught to ask, in effect, "Is this a chair that I see before me?" We observe the chair, but then the existence of the chair is immediately doubted. The chair itself might as easily be any other object of the sense. Even if a chair is the favored object, it does not matter what kind of chair it is. There is no pause here to distinguish an Eames from a Gehry, or to pick out original Mission armchair from a mail-order imitation. All of the furniture in this sleight-of-hand exercise is without distinction, a series of generic macro-objects found lying around and pressed unwittingly into service in a desire for certain and complete knowledge of the world.

As the renegade philosopher Stanley Cavell has shrewdly noted, the disappearing table of skepticism is always just a table, never a Louis XV gilt escritoire. This should give us pause, Cavell says, because it indicates the weirdness—the manufactured quality—of the philosopher's question about knowledge. The question is too general, too comprehensive, to be real; the certainty and generality it seeks to vouchsafe, the Holy Grail of all modern epistemology, is both misleading and dangerous. We would do better, Cavell suggests, to follow our more pedestrian interests. To most normal people, it matters a lot whether the chair before us is a well-restored vintage Deco or just a piece of cheap pine. But in Cartesian-style philosophy, this sort of issue simply never comes up. Furniture disappears as soon as it is called upon the scene. We learn nothing interesting about it: it is merely a handy, non-specific prop that appears only to be routinely destroyed in acts of epistemological experimentation.

This creates a paradoxical situation, for it illuminates both philosophy and furniture. The paradox is that the furniture is annihilated *in general* but must be present *in specific* for the act of annihilation to take place. Descartes had to be sitting somewhere in particular, had to be sitting on something in particular, for him to be able to take the bold step of doubting everything in general. What he can't doubt, in the end, is of course his own act of thinking itself: he thinks, therefore he is. But my point is that he couldn't even do that without a chair.

Function and Beauty

The question in the background here, the unasked philosophical question, is really this one: what is furniture for? That may seem so obvious as to be not worth asking, but one of the things you learn as a philosopher is that the obvious-sounding questions are usually the most interesting ones.

Here is one kind of answer: furniture is for sitting on, lying on, sleeping on, and putting things on. We might call this answer *functionalism,* and it emerges as a common enough version of the Furniture Idea when we force the issue somewhat. Functionalism views furniture as, in effect, an extension of the human ability to com-

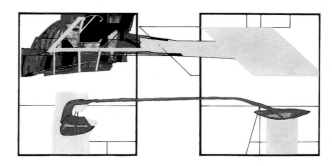

plete manual tasks. Here, for example, is Marshall McLuhan talking about the relationship between furniture and the human body in his book *Counterblast*:

A chair outers the human posterior. The squat position is 'translated' into a new matter, namely wood or stone or steel. The temporary tension of squatting is translated and fixed in a new matter. The fixing of the human posture in solid matter is a great saver of toil and tension. This is true of all media and tools and technologies. But chair at once causes something else to happen that would never

What is furniture for?

occur without a chair. A table is born. Table is a further outering or extension of body resulting from chair. The new fixed posture of chair calls forth a new inclination of body and new needs for the placing of implements and stirring of food. But table also calls forth new arrangements of people at table. The fixing of a posture of the body in a chair initiates a whole series of consequences.

Or, as Burt Bacharach and Hal David more elegantly put it, "A chair is still a chair, even when there's no one sitting there." Notice how McLuhan speaks here of 'chair', 'table', and 'body' as if they were proper names or basic essences, categories rather than things. Notice, too, the causality implied in this kind of functionalism: we squat, therefore we need chairs; we have chairs, therefore we need tables; we have tables, therefore we need place settings.

That is not wrong. Once people begin eating at tables, whole new vistas of social complexity opened up before them. Table manners became an issue, as did the ability to converse while at table. Carving meat in front of others was alone the subject of numerous Renaissance manuals for gentlemen—and still causes anxiety attacks among certain sons-in-law on their first holiday visit. In our own time, the art of throwing the perfect dinner party has become a bourgeois obsession which shows no signs of diminishing in this, the third decade of Martha Stewart's reign.

So functionalism makes a deep point. Furniture arises as the solution to certain problems, as a way of completing certain human tasks—only to create, in the process of so doing, numerous new tasks. It also creates new kinds of aesthetic issues, as Poe reminds us. Any plane surface within a certain range of dimensions, and suspended or supported at a certain height off the floor, may be considered a table. This is the way in which, for example, a philosopher of kinds, natural or non-natural, nominal or real, would speak of tables and chairs. Individual instances are linked together by an articulable essence, consistency with a given design, or certain inductions that can be run, for good reasons, over the class of objects so styled—a good reason being, in this case, something like the combination of cultural and physical factors entailed by "because you can sit in it." But to leave the matter there is to fall into a mundane version of the furniture

demolition of the Cartesian philosopher. Here all tables are equal because they are all merely extensions of our instrumental tasks and bodily dimensions. This misses a deep point about tables. A *good* table isn't just a handy surface or prop; it must also be striking, beautiful, elegant, or witty—or some combination thereof.

These are not functional virtues, they are *aesthetic* ones. But, as is so often the case when it comes to virtue, here aesthetic considerations are not entirely or easily separable from issues of functionality. Any good designer knows that a smooth, highly polished wood surface is both aesthetic and functional; so, depending on your taste,

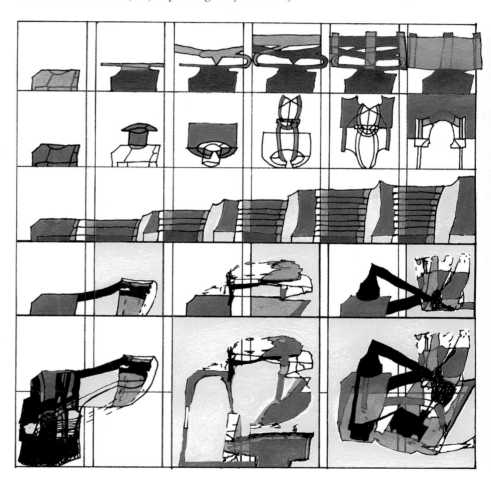

are tapered legs, pediment supports, S-curve lines, high straight backs, and reclining seats. Often enough to be remarkable, the more beautiful thing is also the more useful thing. Functionalism and aestheticism are often thought to be at war, but it would be more accurate to say that they are in creative tension. Rare is the piece of furniture that possesses no aesthetic sense whatsoever, however badly judged. More likely, but still rare, is the piece where aesthetic sense has entirely overwhelmed functionality—though many of us have probably had some near-miss experiences on that score, chairs so beautiful they threaten to pitch you onto the floor at any moment.

Commodity

That is usually as far as most people get when it comes to thinking about the Furniture Idea, but of course there is much more still to say. Furniture is for doing things, and for being beautiful; but it is also for instantiating, illuminating, certain kinds of *political* ideas. In *Das Kapital,* for instance, Marx introduces some insights about the nature of commodities by, as it were, putting a few things on the table. "A commodity appears, at first sight, a very trivial thing and easily understood," he says. And yet: "Analysis shows that in reality it is a very queer thing, abounding in metaphysical subtleties and theological niceties. So far as it is

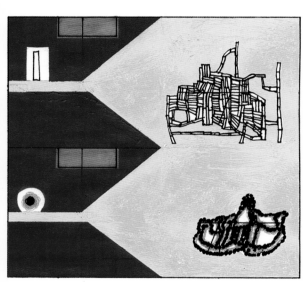

a value in use, there is nothing mysterious about it....The form of wood is altered by making a table out of it; nevertheless, the table remains wood, an ordinary material thing. As soon as it steps forth as commodity, however, it is transformed into a material immaterial thing. It not only stands with its feet on the ground, but, in the face of all other commodities, it stands on its head, and out of its wooden brain it evolves notions more whimsical than if it had suddenly begun to dance." You might think Marx is evolving notions more whimsical than dance-moves right there, but he means that the material thing is now a bearer of non-material significance, of ideological and social payload.

Commodity is not another word for *thing,* it is another word for *relationship.* That is why functionalism and aestheticism, even taken together, cannot tell us all there is to know about a table or chair. The plainest chair is still a product of someone's labor, and was acquired or made against a background of complex social relations determined in large part by money. Every table, from the humblest do-it-yourself kit to the finest handmade piece from, say, Toronto's

Heidi Earnshaw, tells a tale of who owns what. For centuries, furniture has been, along with clothes, hairstyles, companions, leisure activities and personal conveyances, a way of signalling one's place in a complex hierarchy of social relationships, key examples of Erving Goffman's "presentation of self in everyday life." More specifically, it has functioned as what Thorstein Veblen first labeled "invidious comparison" through "conspicuous consumption."

In Veblen's jaundiced view, the messages are not always about what they seem to be about. On the surface, the furnishings of the country house or the high-rise apartment purport to send intricately coded messages of personal taste or sophistication or refinement—and indeed these semiotic codes may well be rooted in some degree of reality. But more basically these objects are purchased, placed, and displayed to indicate, sometimes quite precisely, one's net worth and disposable income. As the critic Adam Gopnik notes, "Veblen is insistent—far more than Marx—on reducing aesthetics to economics." Here's a typical sentence from the early master of consumerist analysis: "The superior gratification derived from the use and contemplation of costly and supposedly beautiful products is," Veblen writes, "a gratification of our sense of costliness masquerading under the name of beauty." Whatever bohemians might like to believe, historically taste is most often just another name for status.

Furniture can also bear political messages in less obvious ways, plotting a new relationship to functionalism. Here, for example, is a passage from Don DeLillo's novel *White Noise,* a scene in which the narrator, a middle-aged Professor of Hitler Studies, catches sight of some undergraduate students scattered in the library of his university, and considers the value of the tuition, $14,000, necessary to attend the elite institution:

> I sense there is a connection between this powerful number and the way the students arrange themselves physically in the reading areas of the library. They sit on broad cushioned seats in various kinds of ungainly posture, clearly calculated to be the identifying signs of some kinship group or secret organization. They are fetal, knock-kneed, arched, square-knotted, sometimes almost upside-down. The positions are so studied they amount to a classical mime. There is an element of overrefinement and

inbreeding. Sometimes I feel I've wandered into a Far Eastern dream, too remote to be interpreted. But it is only the language of economic class they are speaking, in one of its allowable forms.

This studied casualness, this topsy-turvy disdain for the standard operating procedures demanded by chairs and tables, is more than youthful awkwardness. In fact, its outwardly awkward aspect actually hides a deep comfort level, a claim on understanding the way things work, a long acquaintance with the inner machinery of entitlement. Only the truly privileged can lounge so unselfconsciously. Only they can drape themselves over furniture as if furniture has not been fashioned for the human body.

Rearranging the Furniture

All these points are part of what I called the Furniture Idea, but there is at least one further level of meaning alive in tables and chairs. Tables and chairs don't just make us think about function and form and politics. They don't just provide us with the handy platform for our own thoughts. They also make us think about *thinking*.

This happens only where tables and chairs take up their proper places, namely in rooms. And it happens because, as James Agee put it so movingly in *Let Us Now Praise Famous Men,* even the simplest room has the profound grace of human life and everyday aspiration. Writing of the desolate but beautiful homes of Southern sharecroppers that he and photographer Walker Evans examined with such compassion and wisdom, Agee said: "There can be more beauty and more deep wonder in the standings and spacings of mute furnishings on a bare floor…than in any music ever made."

Consider why this is so. Furniture structures space, making what is otherwise undifferentiated into something meaningful. I place a couch in an empty room and it acquires a new significance: the air now shimmers with the possibilities of conversation or napping or seduction. The absent protagonists of the various human stories that room has witnessed and will witness are instantly summoned by the couch's human dimensions, its constant invitation to sit or lie. More than this, though, the couch preserves in its placing the possibility of itself being placed somewhere else: every location of a piece of furniture thus calls attention to all the alternative locations which

have, for the moment, been passed over. We are all attuned to this radiant aspect of furniture, though not all of us can tell immediately when or why a chair is placed oddly or sub-optimally.

The cliché image of what I am getting at here is probably the fickle matron who, moving into a new space, has the exhausted movers try her massive oak-trim settee in every possible location, only to settle back on the very spot where they first dropped it. That image is outdated and maybe offensive, but I think we all share something of this impulse to rearrange the furniture. In Eugene Ionesco's play *The Chairs,* for example, characters enter the stage in order to add more chairs to the scene, each time rearranging and reordering the possibilities (and crises) of the existential situation. It seems to me that we are always doing this, physically or mentally, because we are looking for new ways to structure our allotted space, to make the most of it. We are, in effect, seeking new forms of meaning to create, new ways to think—and new thoughts to entertain. Naturally we can fail to do this well, and then our movements of furniture will be futile, superficial, merely distracting: as the adage has it, we will be rearranging the deck chairs on the Titanic. (A more disturbing contemporary echo of the idea can be found at a website called www.furnitureporn.com, which features photographs of patio and office furniture arranged in various suggestive tableaux. You will never consider swivel chairs the same way again.)

Am I being fanciful? I don't think so. Furniture makes a room what it is, and rooms are where most of us spend most of our time. (Offices, stores, and shops, after all, are rooms too.) How these rooms are furnished, what pieces inhabit them and give them shape, determines in large measure what kinds of thoughts are possible there. This is not just a matter of something like feng shui, though clearly that is one rigorous and ancient way of considering the matter. But consider something that is, for most of us, less exotic: rearranging the furniture in our own room, or even just watching the way the furniture changes as the light does.

In *A la Recherche du Temps Perdu* Proust speaks of the thoughts that come in hazy early morning, when we indulge, he says, "the experimental rearrangement of the furniture in matinal half-slumber." In *The Waves,* Virginia Woolf describes dawn light striking a tree outside her

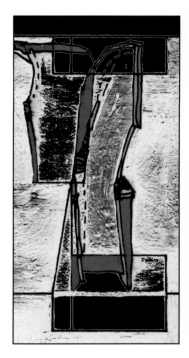

Making what is undifferentiated into something meaningful

window, "making one leaf transparent and then another." At noon, she says, it "made the hills grey as if shaved and singed in an explosion." As afternoon fades, tables and chairs "wavered and bent in uncertainty and ambiguity." And in the evening, the same articles of furniture regain their solidity, so that they are "lengthened, swollen and portentous." Finally, as darkness fell, substance was drained from "the solidity of the hills," and the world was annihilated again.

The style of the furniture itself can be dreamy in this way, reverie-inducing tables and chairs. In *Le Spleen de Paris*, Baudelaire describes such a room as the ideal place to think. "In a prefiguration of Jugendstil," says Walter Benjamin of this project, "Baudelaire sketches 'a room that is like a dream, a truly spiritual room....Every piece of furniture is of an elongated form, languid and prostrate, and seems to be dreaming—endowed, one would say, with a somnambular existence, like minerals and plants.'"

And as with style, so with a particular article of furniture. Gaston Bachelard, in *The Poetics of Space*, focuses on corners and nooks, the parts of a room where, he says, dreams may pool and gather. He likewise favors those items of furniture that enclose space or create inner reaches: "Does there exist a single dreamer of words who does not respond to the word wardrobe?"

he asks. "Every poet of furniture—even if he be a poet in a garret, and therefore has no furniture—knows that the inner space of an old wardrobe is deep. A wardrobe's inner space is also *intimate space*, space that is not open to just anybody." Not all intimate spaces are obvious. For instance, I used to take refuge in the improbable inner space of the clothes hamper with the laundry. I used to think this strange until I discovered that my best friend also did it, and read Salman Rushdie's account, in *Midnight's Children,* of another child who, with perhaps better reason, sought the asylum of the hamper.

In such a room, with such spaces and dreams alive to our gaze, furniture is no longer something merely to sit upon; no longer the elevated surface where we lay our tools and our mealtime places. Here furniture is instead an invitation to think and to dream, a beckoning of possible ideas and half-formed notions. We all sit somewhere when we think, yes, and chairs hold us up while we work out our thoughts on desks and tables. But more importantly, what we sit upon or write upon are themselves as thinking things; not just tools that help us in chosen tasks, but aspects of humanity whose very presence is thought. The attempt of thought to think its own conditions is, as Kant reminds us, infinite and finally impossible: we cannot encompass ourselves within our own reflection. But we can, we must, begin this infinite task anyway, and furniture is one neglected but essential way to do so.

So rearrange the furniture of your ideas by thinking about furniture thinking. The rooms of our existence are throbbing with thoughts waiting to happen, with insights struggling into the ever-changing light. Somewhere right now it is late afternoon, and the midday sun has begun its long fade toward darkness. Or it is early morning and the dawn is slowly, miraculously, illuminating the daily world once more. For a long moment the dim light falls aslant the familiar dimensions of the couch upon which you napped not long ago, or the bedside table that was invisible a moment before, a time impossible to calculate. In the grey light of dawn or dusk, the pieces of furniture appear altered, unfamiliar, slightly threatening—almost alive. The armchair nearby has acquired an air of considered bravado, as if poised for action. The desk stands next to it with an attitude of long-suffering toleration of your many faults. The table glows with boyish anticipation.

Now the light wanes a bit further, and the shapes begin to lose their dimensions—they waver and dissolve. Or the light grows imperceptibly towards its daily intensity, and they take on a new distinctness, an appealing firmness. Stop now, and listen. Listen hard. Listen for the sound of machines for thinking, whispering their thoughts to you. They whisper of love and death and honor lost. They sing of good meals and funny friends and art that moves you. They welcome your achievements and ease your pain. They support you when you can no longer support yourself. They croon and warble and hum. They are the undertones of life. ∎

Fitting In

JONATHAN BINZEN
Text and Photos

Studio furniture finds a home

For four decades now, a woman I know—I'll call her Elizabeth—has been buying furniture from some of the very best studio furniture makers in the country. She has furnished an apartment in Brooklyn and a cottage at the eastern end of Long Island with outstanding pieces by Jere Osgood, Judy McKie, James Krenov, Hank Gilpin, Michael Hurwitz, Bill Walker and perhaps a dozen others. And yet, when you walk into either abode, the immediate feeling is not of entering a gallery or a collection but a home. You might not even notice the furniture at first. What strikes you instead is an atmosphere of comfort and discernment. You find yourself thinking "I want to stay" before you think "I want to look." Soon, however, you begin to see just how extraordinary the furniture is. Somehow, a galaxy of star designers has been coaxed into an ensemble cast.

This coaxing is quite an accomplishment. It is not uncommon for rooms filled with excellent studio furniture to feel discordant and lifeless. It is one thing to select good pieces but quite another to weave them together successfully in a larger composition. Furnishing these rooms has been a life's work, an extended creative act. And like all good art, these rooms are highly personal. But along with the purely personal choices Elizabeth has made, there are a number of more universal elements that help give the rooms their powerful presence.

TRADITION IN CONTEMPORARY FURNITURE **61**

Commissioning creates an elegant space. The dining room of the Brooklyn apartment (shown on pages 61–66) is primarily furnished with pieces made expressly for this room by Jere Osgood, including the ebony table (1966), cherry side chairs (1975), and padauk stereo cabinet (1979). The standing screen (1988) of oak, purpleheart, and ebony is by Geoffrey Warner, and the oak and marquetry cabinet-on-stand (1983) is by Zivko Radenkov (detail, page 61).

Two Paths to Fine Furniture

The same sensibility is expressed inside the apartment and the cottage, yet the two places feel quite distinct. The urban apartment has a unified and formal air, while the cottage in the woods is loose, light, and playful. The differences stem in part from the architecture and in part from the way the two places are used. But the key distinction is that much of the furniture in the apartment was designed expressly for the space by one maker, Jere Osgood. And the furniture in the cottage, by contrast, was made by a range of furniture makers and bought one piece at a time off a gallery floor. There is a great difference between commissioning furniture and acquiring pieces already made, but Elizabeth has clearly been comfortable—and successful—with both ways of buying.

In New York City in the early 1960s, if you wanted to buy handmade furniture and other crafts, you went to America House, the retail store of the American Craft Council. Elizabeth discovered America House soon after moving to the city. She fell in love with a bureau there one day, a contemporary bombe chest in curly mahogany, and she bought it. Some days later, she got a phone call from Jere Osgood. He introduced himself as the chest's maker and then apologized and said he needed the bureau back. He hadn't thought anyone would buy the piece, he explained, and he had committed it to be in a show—could he borrow it? Elizabeth consented, but extracted a promise. In exchange for the favor, he would agree to design a dining table for her. Before too long, she had her Macassar ebony dining table. Some years later, he built chairs to go with it. He also built a tambour sideboard and a stereo cabinet for the dining room and made a dictionary table and lamp table for the living room.

The pieces Osgood made for the apartment show clear evidence of his education in Danish Modern design. The work is clean, straightfor-

wardly functional, and revels in exposed joinery and carefully selected solid wood. But Osgood gives the Danish aesthetic his own particular twist. For a case piece like the maple sideboard, he starts with a rectilinear form, then gives it a puff, inflating it so its sides bow outward. His dining table and chairs are thinned down and harder edged than mainstream Danish Modern furniture. Made with dense, closed-grained woods, they have a buttoned-up beauty that contrasts with the more informal feeling of much Danish Modern furniture.

When Osgood built chairs to go with his dining table, they displaced a set of Hans Wegner chairs in teak and cane, which went out to the cottage. At the extremely spare ebony table, with its rich, dark, sheening surface and stiletto-thin legs, Wegner's caned chairs must have looked nearly rustic. Osgood made the new set of chairs in cherry, which picks up some of the milk-chocolate tones in the ebony. He managed a neat

Danish descent. Osgood's curly maple sideboard (1974) and cherry side chair illustrate the personal interpretation he brings to a powerful tradition.

At the heart of Elizabeth's furniture choices are function and feeling. The detailing of drawer and sliding shelf in Jere Osgood's cherry dictionary cabinet (1977) attract the hand as well as the eye.

trick with these chairs. When they are pulled up to the table, they make a handsome unit with the table, their slender posts and rails tapered and bowed reflecting the movement of the table's legs. But like most of Osgood's furniture, these pieces are comfortable alone as well as in a group. When you leave one of the chairs up against a wall, you see suddenly that with its trapezoidal seat back and line-thin posts it packs a powerful graphic punch.

Osgood's pieces were sensitively scaled to suit the apartment's rooms and taken together they have a reserved elegance—an urbanity—that perfectly suits the place. It is a testament to the modesty of Osgood's work here that even a dozen pieces together don't feel like a monument to one vision. The work is distinctive but still altruistic enough to allow pieces by other makers to look good in the same rooms.

The many pieces Osgood made for the apartment were built over a span of more than two decades using a variety of woods and serving a range of uses. The pieces are diverse enough styl-

istically to keep from blending together, but still they form a coherent whole. This coherence is attributable in part to Osgood's skill and constancy of vision, but it also reflects the strength of his collaboration with Elizabeth. During the years that he was building the restrained pieces for Elizabeth's apartment, Osgood was also designing some far more flamboyant work. Her influence was perhaps responsible for keeping the apartment's furniture in the same key.

Commissioning furniture offers a client great control, but only if the process is driven by good thinking and good drawing. This partnership was blessed with both. Elizabeth could articulate clearly what she wanted from each new piece, and Osgood was expert at interpreting those wishes on paper. As Osgood says of Elizabeth, "She's very sure of what she wants...and she knows what I'm capable of." Osgood remembers that they spent a long time in the drawing phase of each project before proceeding to construction. The time was so productive, Elizabeth says, because Osgood "always produced elegant draw-

Building the sculptural leg structure of Bill Walker's glass and cherry coffee table (1990) required formidable technical skill, but the effort is not evident in the finished piece.

ings. They were spare, but you knew exactly what was going to come."

After this string of successful commissions for her apartment, serendipity and the vagaries of the marketplace brought about a radical shift in the way Elizabeth approached the furnishing of her cottage.

In 1963, when Elizabeth bought Osgood's bombe bureau, only a handful of people in the U.S. were designing and building custom furniture. She was lucky to have found him. And given the paucity of craft furniture for sale, commissioning was the logical thing to do. By the spring of 1981, however, things had changed dramatically. Thanks in part to Osgood himself and others who taught at university-level furniture programs, the field was suddenly bursting with talented young designer/makers. The change was brought home to Elizabeth when she discovered the newly-opened Pritam and Eames Gallery in East Hampton, NY. Here was perhaps the best place in the U.S. to see studio furniture, and it had opened just a few miles from her cottage.

New work by a variety of makers flowed in, one piece at a time. Soon the sea-change in studio furniture was reflected in Elizabeth's cottage. Over the years, as she had commissioned furniture for the apartment, she had simply moved the displaced pieces out to the cottage. She hadn't really thought of the cottage as a place for custom furniture. But now, excited by the flourishing of well-designed furniture, Elizabeth began visiting Pritam and Eames regularly. She didn't make trips there with the idea of buying anything in particular, or buying anything at all, necessarily. But when she saw something she loved—and if she had a place for it—she would buy it. The pieces she bought for the cottage ranged widely, from Hank Gilpin's spare and solid trestle table, a clear statement of function and strength, to James Krenov's delicate cabinet-on-stand, a nuanced exploration of form, texture, and color that retains the function of a cabinet but only vestigially so. She let herself go a little. She bought expressive pieces like Judy McKie's vibrantly carved limewood cabinet and Joe Tracy's can-

An articulate interior speaks several languages. Elizabeth's interests in sculpture, painting, ceramics, woodturning, baskets, plants, and books contribute to a balanced composition in the apartment's living room. The maple armchair (1965) is by Jere Osgood.

tilevered glass-topped coffee table, which is anchored by a large, egg-shaped, sea-washed stone captured in its wooden base.

Buying at the gallery was quite a change from commissioning, but because she was so deliberate about where the pieces would go, Elizabeth was able to bring together pieces by many makers in a pleasing arrangement. In the early 1980s, Elizabeth did commission one piece from a young maker, but she was disappointed with the result and thereafter stuck to buying finished work.

In her two places, Elizabeth managed to have the best of both worlds—a long and fruitful commissioning partnership with one designer, which resulted in an interior of great unity and distilled clarity; and an equally fruitful relationship through a gallery with a range of designers, which resulted in a vibrant and diverse environment drawn together by a deliberate approach to design.

Self-Portrait

The most interesting interiors are revelations of character as well as expressions of taste; they form something of a self-portrait. When Elizabeth was a little girl, her parents bought the first house on their street in the suburbs of Detroit. As other houses rose one after another on lots along the street, Elizabeth became a fascinated spectator. She watched the carpenters closely, intrigued by their hand planing and hand sawing and delighted by the showers and ribbons of fragrant pine they produced. "I got to play with those curls of wood!" she says today, still grateful. She dates her love of things made of wood to that time. Her enduring affection for the material is manifest in the furniture she's bought. The makers whose work she has chosen all respect wood's eloquence. In these pieces, the wood is carefully selected, shown to advantage and finished clear.

By the time she was 20, Elizabeth had absorbed a great deal about design and crafts. Her awareness was stimulated by her group of friends, some of whom studied at the nearby Cranbrook School of Design, which was then in its heyday with designers like Eliel Saarinen, Charles Eames, and Harry Bertoia on the faculty. Elizabeth tried a number of different crafts herself as a young woman. She threw pots, took classes in metalsmithing, even set herself up in her parents' basement and had a go at becoming a metalsmith.

An appreciation for craftsmanship flowed naturally out of these experiences, and it is apparent in the furniture she has chosen. From Joe Tracy's coffee table to Jere Osgood's curly maple sideboard, these are all pieces that bear evidence of the process of being made. All is exposed: joinery, wood grain, and the structure of the piece. All, that is, except the struggle behind the finished design. Elizabeth does not seem to favor virtuoso exploration of technique. A piece like Bill Walker's round coffee table certainly required great technical skill, but the design is so well resolved that its strongest statement is about form rather than technique; here and in other pieces she has chosen to live with, the technique remains implicit rather than becoming explicit.

A love of the tactile was part of what drew Elizabeth to making things herself, and a richly tactile experience is something she seeks in furniture. From James Krenov's cabinet on stand to James Schriber's nightstand, Elizabeth's pieces all invite the touch. They've got subtly textured surfaces and beautifully articulated joints. No sleek, squared-off, opaque-lacquered cabinets here.

In her mid 20s, Elizabeth saved her money, quit her job in journalism, and took a solo trip to Scandinavia. Much of the best design was coming out of Scandinavia, and she wanted to see it in person. She spent time in Denmark, going from shop to gallery to museum, drinking it all in, and then went on to Sweden. She couldn't afford to buy furniture on that trip, but it hardly mattered. The impact of what she saw would stay with her as tangibly as if she had returned with a houseful of furniture.

This first-hand education in Scandinavian design laid perhaps the perfect groundwork for an appreciation of American studio furniture. The links between Scandinavian Modern and contemporary American furniture are many. Scandinavian Modern furniture was everywhere in the U.S.

in the 1950s and 1960s and had a pervasive influence on popular taste in furniture. Most contemporary American studio furniture makers probably grew up with such furniture in their houses. But the connections were even more direct. Nearly every one of the makers whose work Elizabeth has bought studied furniture making in Denmark or Sweden or has learned from someone who did.

James Krenov studied under Swedish designer Carl Malmsten and worked in Sweden for 25 years. Krenov went on to teach hundreds of American furniture makers, four of whom have exemplary work in these rooms: Bill Walker, Zivko Radenkov, Ted Hawke, and Paul Harrell. Almost all the other makers represented here were taught by Tage Frid or by one of Frid's students. Frid was born and trained in Denmark before spending some 45 years as a teacher and writer in the U.S.

Elizabeth's cottage presents many fine juxtapositions. (Photos of this interior are on pages 67–71.) Here, a massproduced metal bench contrasts with James Krenov's warm and highly personal cabineton-stand (1983).

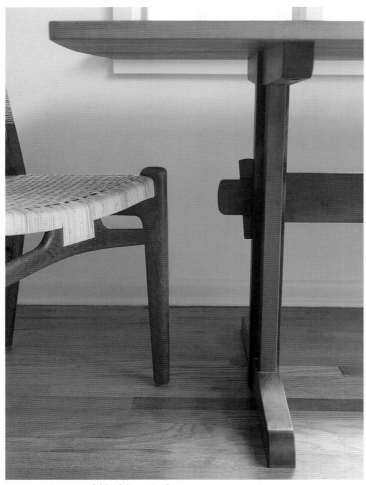

Arranged kinships. Hank Gilpin's forthright trestle table (1982) mates perfectly with Hans Wegner's dining chairs, both eloquently expressing their structure. At right, an oil painting by Jane Wilson and a spare grouping of ceramics complement Judy McKie's carved limewood cabinet (1984).

Hank Gilpin, Geoffrey Warner, and Jere Osgood all studied under Frid. Osgood went on to study for a year in Denmark himself and then returned to the U.S. and taught many others, including James Schriber and Michael Hurwitz.

Some years after her first trip, Elizabeth returned to Denmark and bought a set of Hans Wegner dining chairs. She still uses them in the cottage; with their simply expressed structure, solid-wood craftsmanship, and exposed joinery, these mass-produced chairs stand squarely in the same aesthetic stream as the custom-made furniture that flows around them.

Balance and Structure

These interiors are not all about furniture, and it's a good thing. Elizabeth's eye is engaged also by paintings, sculpture, books, baskets, ceramics, turned objects, plants, fabrics, and all sorts of curious things she's found on walks: shells, stones, pods, and other fragments of nature, which she arranges in still lifes with an artist's finesse. The evenhanded way the furniture and all these other objects are integrated creates an essential balance:

the overall environment is strengthened because its constituent elements are given their just space and no more. Those still lifes of picked-up pieces are microcosms of the interiors—each arrangement of little objects is seemingly casual but embodies a sophisticated sense of composition in its interplay of shapes, textures, and colors.

A similar balance obtains among the pieces of furniture. Variations in quality, detailing, and materials between the pieces seem to clarify the characteristics of each. Elizabeth mixes custom furniture and well-designed production pieces with some fairly ordinary department store stuff. The humbler pieces, most of them sofas and upholstered chairs, keep the overall tone in these rooms from becoming uncomfortably elevated. Wang Shixiang, in his book *Classic Chinese Furniture,* speaking of the effect of rarified furniture, says "three or four pieces will transform a room, and it is best to limit the pieces to this number in order to allow the real spirit of the furniture to communicate itself. If more pieces are crowded in one room, the effect will be entirely spoilt." Elizabeth clearly understands this idea.

Buying each piece of furniture for a specific place in her cottage, Elizabeth successfully blends work by a range of makers. In the foreground an asymmetric Osgood side table (1998) flanks a Wegner chair.

Ted Hawke's birdseye maple jewelry box (1987) is sophisticated casework on an intimate scale. James Schriber's shapely nightstand (1997) in curly maple, sycamore, and holly, reinterprets classical forms.

In both the cottage and the apartment, the upholstered pieces are plainly built for comfort. Big and soft and blocky, they provide a contrast to the slender-limbed, sinuous hardwood pieces around them. In the cottage, for example, there is a pair of sofas bought 30 years ago at Design Research. There is nothing special about them. With flat side panels, squared cushions, and floral print fabric, they are a bit clunky. But surrounded as they are by finely detailed, highly resolved designs, the settees provide a welcome respite, a needed touch of awkwardness that helps anchor the elegance around them.

A handful of production pieces occupies the middle ground between the solid-wood studio furniture and the upholstered pieces, and they serve to introduce further contrasts that heighten one's appreciation of all the furniture. A circular gray stone side table in the living room of the cottage stands between two Wegner chairs. With its rich, dark color and cool, flaked surface, the stone table provides a beautiful counterpoint to the warm, slender, burnished wood beside it. In the entrance hall of the cottage, a black wrought metal settee stands beside a James Krenov cabinet-on-stand. The Krenov piece is warm, interpretive, and organic, attracting the touch; the settee, by contrast, is cool, deliberate, and geometric. Proximity enhances each.

Elizabeth will tell you she is not a collector. She has never bought pieces to fill gaps in a collection—for the sake of having a Hurwitz, say. Pieces haven't been bought in a burst of impractical enthusiasm and then fitted in wherever enough room could be found. Rather, she has bought studio furniture much the way one would buy furniture at Ikea or the department store—to fill needs in her house. Nearly every piece of studio furniture she has bought replaced something else, typically something storebought, something functional but not distinguished—"newlywed furniture," as she puts it. Every new piece has a given place in the overall composition and is quickly woven into the larger fabric.

As a result, the arrangement of these rooms feels familiar. Over the years of buying and replacing furniture, a structure developed based on how the rooms flow and function best. And the soundness of that structure communicates itself as a kind of intuitive familiarity and comfort. The furniture here is not atypically arranged, it is simply atypically good.

Joe Tracy used a tide-washed chunk of granite he found to anchor his cantilevered pearwood and glass coffee table (1986). Elizabeth understands the impulse; evidence of her love of gardening and walking is seen in many arrangements of small found objects throughout the cottage.

Modesty

Furniture making is a social art. A dialogue in physical form between maker and user; between use and grace. And in this respect, furniture is unchanging. The demands of function draw a direct line between the furniture makers of classical antiquity and those working today. Now as then, the furniture maker's challenge is to give elegant expression to human need. Furniture consecrates use.

On one level, this is uncontroversial. But on another, it is open to debate. In the last decades of the twentieth century, many makers of handmade furniture began to flout the demands of function and veer off in the direction of sculpture. Just as avant garde art in the twentieth century had evolved into something resembling philosophy—scrapping the search for beauty in favor of a search for meaning—some avant garde furniture making turned away from function and toward unfettered self-expression.

This more sculptural furniture, or metafurniture, can be exciting in a photo or in a gallery but frustrating as a dining table. In this work, the traditional dialogue between use and aesthetics, between user and maker, has become more or less a monologue on the part of the maker. By abandoning function, or downplaying it, meta-furniture gains artistic freedom but loses its entrée into the heart of daily life.

The studio furniture Elizabeth has bought is at once traditional and progressive. It is progressive in seeking new techniques and forms, and traditional in placing function at the center of the design equation. Even the most expressive of her pieces call out to be used, and this is key to the success of the spaces. Every piece she bought was earmarked to go in a particular place and to serve a specific function, and this has kept the spaces from becoming a clash of egos.

Elizabeth does have a taste for more expressive furniture as well. "If I had more room," she says, "I'd probably have more sculptural stuff." When she does get a piece that edges off toward pure expression, she finds a place to put it—a hall or vestibule, for instance—where the burden of function is naturally reduced.

The pieces in these rooms nearly all show their makers in top form. But they don't ring of the magnum opus. Selecting pieces "that I want to look at, things that soothe me," Elizabeth has instinctively picked great furniture that would yet be amenable to being blended in with other excellent work. There's a quality Elizabeth shares with her furniture.

I'd call it modesty. ■

A Meditation on the Desk

JERE OSGOOD

New forms for familiar functions—reflections on one of the most personal furniture forms from a maker and teacher who has been a quiet leader in the field

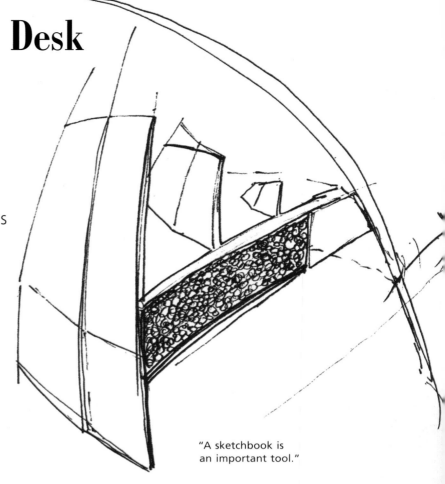

"A sketchbook is an important tool."

When I was teaching, we talked about there being three times in the life of a piece: first is designing the piece, second is making the piece, and third is responding to it. The difficulty and the rewards of the second phase are very important to me. I participate in the making of the piece, and that experience can't be sold. You can't give it away. But to me it's the reason for doing it. In many ways it's more valuable than the piece itself.

Sometimes I hurry the design and drawing time so I can get to that middle time. When I was teaching full-time I kept saying how important it was to follow through with the design, not to change it too many times, because students need to build up a visual vocabulary. Even if the piece is wrong, you can learn from completing it.

Drawing

I often don't finish the whole drawing before beginning construction. I tend to go fast through the drawing stage in order to get to the building stage. I may wait to see some section, then do more drawings to visualize the details, or I work things out in a pine mock-up. The piece may not have come into focus yet, and I keep producing new drawings as I work from the outside in. On the interior of a desk, for instance, I'll often need to experience the piece as a full-size form, and then I can design the rest quite quickly.

Design and Vision

I'm fascinated by the separate components of a piece. They often get me into a project, though I don't design around components. It's really the other way around. I'm likely to feel or sense the whole form before working out the various elements. A vision happens occasionally, or I dream of a form. It's a way of looking around corners, a hint of feelings to come. I'm sure it's also an accumulation from past encounters.

A sketchbook is an important tool, something you stress as a teacher, like a mantra—keep a sketchbook, keep a sketchbook.

Architecture, Scale, and Identity

The training I had as an architect gave me the design tools that were never addressed while I was studying furniture making at the Rochester Institute of Technology (RIT). I went there with a design/problem-solving system that still guides my work. The interior of my "Spring Desk" looks very architectural, like cliff dwellings.

I was thrilled the first time someone asked me what this desk was, because it meant that it

Photos of desks, except where noted: Dean Powell

didn't fit their preconceived idea of a desk. I think if we can do something that doesn't have a readily recognizable reference to it, that's a breakthrough. Scale is an important reference. If you look at a drawing or a finished piece and you can't immediately identify it as a desk because you can't tell whether it's three feet or six feet, then that to me means something successful about the design. It's not immediately plugged into an associative value structure. What I try to do is to create new forms within the familiar constraints of function. Without the constraints the danger is that you become too sculptural. But I'm too conservative for that.

I worked a long time on the composition of the side. I don't always get the stance right, sometimes I'm happier with it than other times, but this one probably has the strongest sense of stance of any of my desks.

"The interior looks very architectural, like cliff dwellings." Spring Desk (1996), bubinga, wenge, 51"h x 49"w x 32"d.

tesy Currier Gallery of Art; gift of Edward and Hilda Fleisher, the Joan Dunfey Fund, Dr. and Mrs. Huntington Breed II, Kimon and Anne Zachos, and the Friends.

"Opening or closing
the doors becomes
a theatrical event."
Tall Desk (1995),
figured cherry,
77"h x 35"w x 26"d.

Silhouette and Detail

My "Tall Desk" is an imposing piece. Opening or closing the doors becomes a theatrical event. They're more than four feet tall and curved across their width. They disappear into the cabinet when opened. Important here, as in much of my work, is the silhouette of the piece when you come upon it in a room. As you get closer, you'll see some more detail in addition to the profile. You'll see the pattern of the wood. Once you get very close, that disappears and you pick up on the structural detail. As your attention shifts, it's very important that there be something there. A lot of antique pieces overdo that. They rely on close-proximity amazement. They try to trick you into believing it's a very fine piece when from fifteen feet away it may have abysmal proportions. They get caught up in marquetry or inlaid gold birds. My pieces are simple on the outside, but I try to provide good close-up detail, whether it's in the figure of the wood, the shape of the components, or the detailing.

First Desk

I made my first desk for the 1958 Young Americans show, the "Competitive Exhibition of the American Craftsmen's Council." Wharton Esherick was one of the jurors, and Wendell Castle had a piece in the 1962 show that got him a lot of attention. It was a show for people under 30; I was a first-year student at RIT at the time. It has a 6-inch-wide fall-down front and a top that folds open. It's a standard Victorian design that came from a desk I saw at my aunt's house—she had a lot of antiques—and I thought I could do better. It's impractical, but it's a nice simple design. I'd seen that kind of turned leg somewhere and liked the idea that the taper could be curved rather than straight. Turning was natural for me because my father and grandfather had a lathe and turned all the time.

Second Desk

My second desk was more formal and shows an influence from Tage Frid, who was my teacher at RIT. He encouraged me with the tambours and the complex joinery, though the idea for the piece came from things I was seeing in magazines. His work was straighter. I did this desk at the beginning of my graduate studies, which I didn't continue. The desk functions pretty well. The tambour in the bottom curves inward to create space for your knees, and there's a pull-out work surface. So I was becoming aware of what's supposed to happen functionally in a desk. But I didn't get the cubbyholes right. They aren't deep enough for long envelopes, and the upper tambour won't shut with them in. I always remember that. If I see someone doing a desk, I remind them to measure and be sure.

Osgood's first desk was a student project (1958), walnut, silver, 31"h x 30"w x 16"d.

His second desk explores tambours and complex joinery (1960), walnut, leather, 48"h x 44"w x 20"d.

First Elliptical Desk

Before my first elliptical shell desk, I'd done dining tables and chests of drawers, but I didn't start on these desks until the late 1960s. There was a horseshoe-shaped desk that I made before this one, but it had straight legs. That taught me to begin thinking about the pedestal to support a curved form.

I also realized here that the desk was a place for composition. I was fascinated by the shell form. That came from helping someone make a lute. At the time I thought the way to develop pure form was to follow elliptical mathematical formulas. In the late 1950s through the 1960s when I was doing things for America House (the craft store in New York City), I was turning plates to catenaries, carefully following pure mathematical formulas. With this elliptical shell I realized it was better not to use a pure mathematical form. There are so many interesting or profound things that can happen by drawing the lines freehand or tracing them with a bent stick. You draw on irrational quirks that we all have. Those little things that are personally yours are most important for your work as an artist. You should ask

"...thinking about the pedestal to support a curved form." Elliptical Shell Desk (1970), walnut, ash, curly maple, 48"h x 53"w x 38"d.

"...so many interesting or profound things that can happen by drawing the lines freehand." Elliptical Shell Desk (1992), bubinga, wenge, birdseye maple, 45"h x 50"w x 34"d. Side Chair, Santa Clara walnut. In background: Ceramic Bench by Nisha Crawley, Barbara Campbell, Dan Ferguson.

Rick Mastelli

yourself when you're making something, what can I contribute to this that is distinctly my own? If I take and use a pure elliptical form, I may be bonding to the cosmos or something, but it's not expressing lines that I alone should say.

I think the interior of this one is awful! I'm embarrassed by it because it's so static. If you compare this early "Shell Desk" to one of the later ones, which can look like an organ loft or something, you see how conventional this first one is. I'd gotten somewhere with the overall form, but I didn't understand yet the importance of relating the interior to it.

Also, this desk opens with the lid moving inside the back. On later desks the opening section moves on the outside of the back. That's a much better system. If you put papers where the section opens inside, it'll bend them, and pencils can get jammed in there.

The legs aren't bad. I haven't changed those much over the years. I think I can do them with more feeling now, but it's a small difference. These legs were rounded over along the edges by running a router up and down them. Now I wouldn't bring a router within a hundred yards of those legs.

Why Laminates

It's important to me to recognize and follow the inherent qualities of wood as a furniture material. Lamination, the way I use it, follows the growth patterns in a tree better than can be achieved with traditional joinery techniques using square milled-to-thickness lumber. I don't try to hide the laminations on the edges. I'm not trying to disguise the technique. I developed my techniques by searching in the design stage for new forms that would be strong and have a sense of freedom. It's a high-tech process that aims for a natural result.

Years after developing the technique, I was going through an old book and came across a black-and-white photo of a tree form that looks like my leg forms—the shape and the lines. It must have been in my mind, because I know I had that book long before I did the laminations.

For the first tapered legs I made, I thickness-planed $1/4$- or $5/16$-inch layers and laminated them into a curve. Then I bandsawed the taper through the gluelines. Not only did I get all these unsightly gluelines, but it was weak. And so a light went on—taper the laminations and eliminate bandsawing through the gluelines!

Osgood ponders clamping procedures on his latest Elliptical Shell Desk, this one with a segmented top that opens in two halves, pivoting on a vertical axis. At left, a page from the book *Anatomy of Nature* by Andreas Feininger (Crown, 1956) may have inspired Osgood's lamination technique.

"A number of my desks have been displayed in the middle of a room." Elliptical Shell Desk (1992). In the background are a table and chairs by Bill Walker, a low chest by Kristina Madsen, a chest by Rick Wrigley, and Osgood's Standup Desk (see also page 82).

All Sides of a Piece

I work from all sides of a piece—at the sketch stage, the large-scale design stage, and the pilot model stage. And they're finished so that you can see both sides. None of them has a back of stapled fir plywood, as if it's going to go against the wall. Even the "Tall Desk" (page 74), which does go against a wall, has a gentle convex curved back. That to me looks like a finished piece of furniture.

A number of my desks have been displayed in the middle of a room, and I get tangled up in the language of it—I can't talk about the back and the front. I have to say the side you sit at or the side you don't sit at, to keep the vocabulary straight. One way of using them is to put the end against the wall.

Evoking Concept through Form

I've heard this "Dome Desk" described as looking like a biomorphic creature, with a head and legs. It does have a sort of brainy character. Some desks are about the relationship of people on either side of it. This one is more about you and it, and then the interior. Like most pieces that open and close, it's really a dual form.

Some people see the tendrils of a jelly fish in the legs, but I'd say if it was anything, it was tree forms, tree roots. But I also try to create a sense of animation, or at least a posture that's poised for movement. I'm very conscious of that and I'll play with it in my pine models.

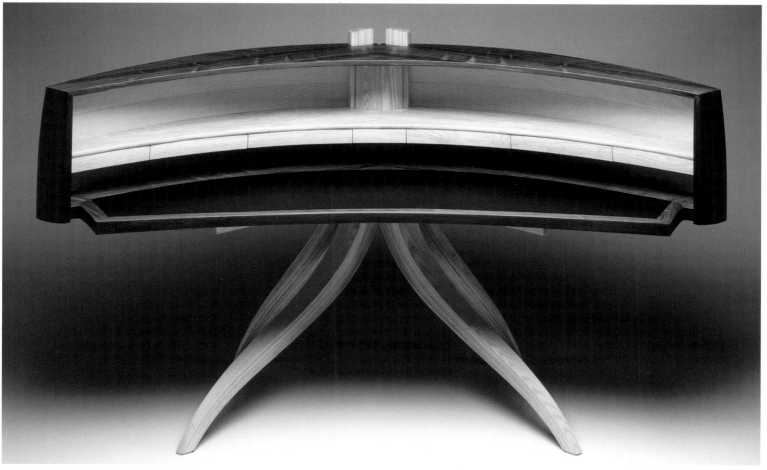

"As with many of my desks, to sit at it is to complete the form."
Brazilian Rosewood and Ash Desk (1985), 45"h x 80"w x 34"d.

"If it was anything, it was tree forms." Dome Desk (1985),
bubinga, wenge, 66"h x 50"w x 30"d.

Why Desks

I like to do desks because they're a good composition field.
A chest of drawers is a more even, closed form—you can
look at it with a drawer open, but that's it. With a desk
you can get views of it as a closed form, flat planes and
outlines in the working surface, structure and detailing of
the interior, the relationship of the interior to the exterior—there's a variety of possibilities. It's a more dynamic
form, and I'm always interested in exploring it. If a gallery
asks me for something, I'll say, "Oh, how would you like
a desk?"

I'm interested in how you use furniture, and the desk
is particularly good for this. This "Brazilian Rosewood and
Ash Desk" is almost 7 feet long, and I remember very
specifically forming its lines by sitting at a big table and
getting all the reach lines and practicing with a pile of
papers here and a pile there, how comfortable was the
shelf to access or to look over. I may have even put a
piece of plywood down with a piece of tracing paper over
it. I do things like that to work out the function.

I shape all the forms. The gentle curving and doming
is an attempt to follow an organic principle responding to
the human form—because we aren't flat or square. People have said it looks like the piece is presenting itself, as
if to be of service, as if it's in a curtsy. As with many of
my desks, to sit at it is to complete the form. I do try to
get people closer to the furniture.

"The piece appears to move as you walk around it."
Top: Laminated Ash Desk (1987), ash, leather, 32"h x 72"w x 26"d.
Above: Guild Desk (1992), Santa Clara walnut, 29"h x 58"w x 22"d.
Right: Writing Desk (1986), bubinga, ash, 31"h x 59"w x 22"d.

Movement and Peripheral Vision

You're really missing the experience of these cantilevered desks in person. The images are incredibly flat compared to the real objects. Each piece appears to move as you walk around it, so it's not just how you use it, but how you perceive it as you encounter at it as an object. You can't do that with a photograph. I wanted the curve of the cantilevered top to appear to move in relation to you. And it does.

I don't mean, jump two feet. Just that if you walk by it and you're looking at one point, other points seem to shift. I've found that if you can see a curve in your peripheral vision, it's almost a subconscious thing. It will shift or roll. I've asked people about this over the years and they say, yes, it does happen.

It may have to do with the shape of your path as you walk around the desk and the difference between that shape and the shape of the top. If you think about your eye moving in a different pattern—your eye can't be moving along the exact curve of the desk, or the curve would appear flat—the relationship between the two shapes is necessarily a dynamic one.

Our primary field of vision is about 20 degrees. It's slightly different with glasses and a whole list of things that influence it. But we can see well beyond that narrow field through peripheral vision. Peripheral vision strongly affects our sense of things. You can register how significant it is by looking through a tube, which eliminates it.

When a piece is large enough to engage our peripheral vision, it involves not just sight but also the brain, and you become more interactive with it. Unlike with something small, a piece of jewelry, for example, you have to do more processing in order to proportionally incorporate its different elements. It's like needing to have a conversation with the object, a back and forth, because it's bigger, more extensive, than can be apprehended in one moment. That's why I don't like little scale models of furniture. You get them in one shot, whereas with a six-foot mock-up of a desk, you have to scan it. It's more of an experience. You shouldn't try to sell a full-size desk from a three-inch model. It's a different visual experience.

On the other hand, it's also important to remember how people sort of touch things with their eyes. And it's not just with their eyes! I want people to touch the edge and trace the curve on a piece. It's an adventure for me, how that happens. What you want is that people will let it happen. If they see a piece in a museum or a gallery, they need to pause long enough for this back-and-forth experience to happen, to have a conversation with the piece.

Controlling Tension

As I continue to explore this form, I've varied the relationship between the legs and the top. I first made the basic design of the 1992 "Guild Desk" in 1981 (that desk was featured on the back cover of *Fine Woodworking* in July 1982). In this design the legs stop below the surface of the top. It's a more relaxed effect compared to that of the 1986 desk, where the space between the legs is carried up and the legs are mitered into the backboard (I call it the wings), creating more graphic impact. There's a tension and release as the legs come together and spread out.

With the desk I did in 1987, the legs join into a central stalk, which looks more organic, I think. And you also have the angled ends of the legs visible from the top of the desk. This central stalk design has been an odd one to work on. It's not stable, it won't stand up until the top is on. Yet, when you put the top on and set it all on the floor, it's not going to fall over. I'm planning to go back to the central stalk again. I'm intrigued by that structure and form.

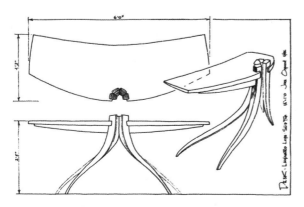

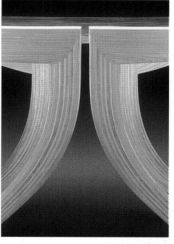

Controlling tension through the years: At top (1992, revisiting the earliest variation on this design that dates back to 1981), the legs come together and terminate below the surface of the desk. Center (1986), the legs remain separate and are mitered into the backboard, creating a strong graphic tension. At right (1987), the legs join one another at an angle along their length into a more organic-looking stalk.

A Conservative Piece

For the "Nantucket Desk" I was working with a conservative client. And to me that meant I shouldn't even think of a pedestal base but rather four legs positioned more conventionally. The lines on those legs look like they have direct historical reference, maybe Hepplewhite. But I was trying to pick up on the feeling you get from Nantucket, where the desk was going into the client's home office. I've been to Nantucket a number of times, and you can't get very far from the water or boats there. So that led to this modified shiplap on the sides and back, and the wave line on the top and skirt. The client liked it, and I thought it was a good accommodation of both the conservative requirements and my expressive interests.

Wharton Esherick

For this "Standup Desk" I was influenced by Wharton Esherick, whose place I visited after he'd died. All furniture students should go there. It's important to see what he did. When I saw his work in New York City in the 1950s, I felt like it gave me permission to do what I wanted to do. Up to that point I'd been exposed only to factory furniture. He did that amazing thing for me, gave me permission early in my career.

"I was trying to pick up on the feeling you get from Nantucket." Nantucket Desk (1992), East Indian rosewood, 41"h x 60"w x 33"d.

Subtlety and Complexity

I don't know if you can see it, but there are lamination lines coming up from the legs all the way to the top of the side of this "Shell Desk." I made an extra leg, continuing the laminations, and sliced it into veneer so I could carry these flow lines on the surface of the side—it's a marquetry pattern that continues the structure. The brass pivot has the same tree-like shape. When you look at the desk, the lines in the side are not readily apparent. But if you keep looking, you sense them out of the corner of your eye. So you feel them more than see them, and that's what I wanted, to keep it subtle.

It's a complex piece with a lot of things going on, like extending the tree-like brass pivot past the axis. I did that for visual balance.

The line at the bottom of the drawer—to me it's sort of an intense counterpoint. There are simple lines throughout the piece, and if you run a simple line along for a while, it's good to just jiggle it and then settle it down again. That jiggle is meant to be visual, but also tactile. People will touch it, or feel as if they're touching it.

I learned about the power of touch when I was making accessories in the 1960s. I did accessories as small compositions, but you can't participate with your body as much with a bookend as you can with furniture. I appreciated the detail, the delicacy, of doing accessories. It wasn't that I turned my back on them. I just wanted more. ■

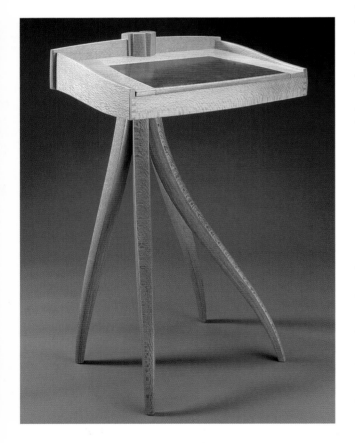

"I was influenced by Wharton Esherick....it gave me permission to do what I wanted to do." Standup Desk (1997), Australian lacewood, leather, 47"h x 30"w x 21"d.

In the collection of the Rhode Island School of Design Museum

"People will touch it, or feel as if they're touching it." Shell Desk (1999), bubinga, wenge, Ceylonese satinwood, leather, brass, 44"h x 43"w x 31"d.

Art Furniture

KATHRAN SIEGEL

Poised precariously
between fine art and
fine furniture

Art furniture resists definition, resting somewhere between two traditions: fine art and
fine furniture. What is valued highly as
art has little, if any, value as fine furniture,
and the same is true in reverse. While fine
furniture seeks to be accommodating and the
embodiment of good design, fine art values the
idiosyncratic and unsettling, at least in our time.
This conflict has been problematic among scholars and collectors of art furniture, whose larger
ambitions include determining its value. It is,
however, precisely in this lack of possible resolu-
tion that the significance of art furniture lies.

Whether we choose to consider a chair as fine
art or as fine furniture, we are challenged by the
other set of standards. This conceptual discomfort
is at the heart of what makes art furniture so
compelling. The art furniture maker is forced to
confront choices about his work which cause it
to fall, in varying degrees, on one or the other

side of the divide. As the audience, we are
brought to reconsider furniture conventions that
have long gone unquestioned.

When discussing the work of art furniture
makers, it is productive to examine this unstable
marriage of two traditions as a way of determining meaning, or content, rather than in an attempt
to discredit the work. Meaning, itself being a condition of this partnering of fine art and fine furniture, is always a component and, as such, an
important consideration when evaluating each
individual work. Art furniture makers who consider themselves to be artists feel compelled to
choose a side—art or furniture? The true significance of art furniture gets lost in such a question,
which rests upon the assumption that a choice can
be made at all. Being an artist appears to be more
open to self-definition than being a furniture
maker. But, in truth, the art world flatly denies
the credibility of art furniture. And traditional furniture makers are just as unwelcoming.

Function

Function is one consideration that might help
sort things out. As a subgroup within the studio furniture movement, art furniture makers
approach function in the service of some expressive interest. In this regard they are connected to
the tradition of fine arts. The work of individual
makers is easy to identify since each works out
of a personal vocabulary that is somewhat idiosyncratic and thus self-defining. This is a quality
typically found among fine artists but not uncommon among fine furniture designers either. Just
consider Thonet or Marcel Breuer, Philippe Starck
or Shiro Kuramata. Among art furniture makers
this vocabulary may be representational, like
Craig Nutt's vegetables, or abstract, like Paul
Freundt's sweeping planes poised upon animated
tubular legs.

Work that draws upon earlier art movements
such as Surrealism, with its taste for biomorphic
abstraction and its practice of juxtaposing elements
out of context, is easy to find in art furniture, particularly among those makers, such as Joël Urruty,
whose forms embed function within fanciful
imagery. In much of the furniture Mitch Ryerson
designs, found objects are worked seamlessly into
the structure; sometimes they are simulated,
rendered to look like found objects but
made of other materials. When an old

Pat Simione

Among art furniture makers a personal vocabulary—whether abstract or representational—is often idiosyncratic and therefore self-defining.
Above: Craig Nutt, "Celery Chair with Carrots, Peppers and Snow Pea" (1992), wood, leather. Left: Mitch Ryerson, "Handyman Special" (2000), birch, basswood, maple, lead flashing, milk paint, gold leaf, 68"h. Below: Paul Freundt, "Etruria" (1998), fabricated steel with patina. Facing page: Joël Urruty, "Head of Drawers" (2000), mahogany, milk paint, 84"h.

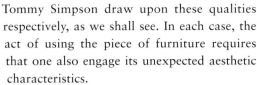

meaning is recycled or imitated, a new meaning results. Along with new meaning, the juxtaposed object continues to carry vestiges of its old familiarity. This double association enriches our experience. One is reminded of the earlier sculptures by Pablo Picasso where, for example, a bicycle seat and handlebars are transformed into a bull's head. Furniture makers use other established forms of abstraction as well. The early work of Jay Stanger borrowed a Constructivist language which he has since made his own. On the side of realism, Garry Knox Bennett has borrowed from Pop Art, and Tom Eckert from Photo Realism as well as from the earlier tradition of *trompe l'oeil* still life.

Studio furniture is largely representative of the sensibility of an individual maker. When this sensibility is unique, the resulting work bears some relationship to art. It is a matter of degree. At the opposite end, when the interest is to replicate traditional designs, then the relationship is to craft alone. Unique within the world of craft as art, which feels obliged to eliminate functionality in the service of art, art furniture makers often exploit function. Because of its interactive potential, art furniture often carries a performative value that can translate into an art experience when it conveys something ritualistic, ceremonial, or narrative. Furniture engages the whole physical self in its use, so it is especially suited to these types of expressive content. Works by Keith Crowder, Wendy Maruyama, and

Is the means of production enough to distinguish industrial design from functional sculpture? Above: Wharton Esherick, "Music Stand" (1962), walnut, cherry (courtesy Wharton Esherick Museum). Below: Ray and Charles Eames, "La Chaise," manufactured by Vitra (1991–present), plastic, chrome steel, wood.

Tommy Simpson draw upon these qualities respectively, as we shall see. In each case, the act of using the piece of furniture requires that one also engage its unexpected aesthetic characteristics.

There are many junctures where the art furniture maker must decide the degree to which he will commit himself to one tradition or the other. Good furniture design is usually still a case of form following function. Within that parameter a designer has some freedom to develop a style, or vocabulary, but this too will be in the service of utility. An aesthetic object, on the other hand, will forgo some functionality for the sake of its expressive quality. Thus decisions need to be made all along the way concerning the extent to which one set of standards will be superseded by the other.

Good Design and Beauty

An Eames chair exhibits good design because it solves the problem of comfort and good looks efficiently, using an economy of means. Applying modern industrial technology, Ray and Charles Eames made their designs affordable to consumers. Design that is good as such is different from the good design of Wharton Esherick, who sculpted his free-form pieces of furniture individually, by hand, using traditional woodworking techniques. Esherick had a different expectation—his work was personal and retained a strong sculptural reference.

In an Eames chair, beauty resides in the invention of a formal solution that is direct, economical, and aesthetically pleasing. Esherick, on the other hand, had a primary interest in making beautiful forms, and in exposing the natural beauty of the material itself. His concept of beauty emulated the values of traditional sculpture. His work expressed a desire to incorporate function into the aesthetic experience. Good design is then defined to be the result of a give-and-take between these two sets of criteria.

The problem, stated another way, is how to marry these two traditions. Because Esherick's interests included the clearly formal, this marriage was easier than it would be for a furniture maker who wished to add personally expressive content in the form of some message. Formal expression still remains about the work itself. The maker plays the role of facilitator or conduit between

Courtesy Vitra Design Museum

the material and the final form it will take. When the maker's interest is in personal expression, then both the material and the final form it takes are in the service of something removed from the work itself—an idea. This is a difficult assignment for a piece of furniture, which still has to explain why it needs to be furniture at all.

In traditional fine arts, beauty is often described as a transcendent quality set in motion by a complex arrangement, or design, consisting of visual and associative events generated by the work of art. Sculptors less than a century ago still worked their materials only to the point of revealing a magnificence they believed to reside within the material itself, not unlike the way Michelangelo worked. It was their job to make this quality visible. But today "truth to material" is only one of many approaches. Beauty, in any form, is no longer necessarily a desired byproduct of fine art, though it is of good design. Fine artists have grown suspicious of beauty's seductive quality. They view it as a strategy to be exploited only in the service of an appropriate idea. In its place, much contemporary art is presented "raw," which, predictably, has developed into an aesthetic of its own.

Function for What?

Though function has traditionally marked the divide between art and design, functionality has been an ongoing topic among fine artists since early in the twentieth century. The difference between design objects and sculpture today has little to do with function per se. Instead, the question needs to be asked, "Function in the service of what?" When function is used to convey an idea, or some expressive content, then an object is likely to fall on the side of sculpture. When function is in the service of some utility, or of some expedience, then we evaluate it in terms of design.

Gerrit Rietveld, famous for his "Red Blue Chair," became a leading member of the de Stijl movement of the 1920s and 1930s, which is associated with rectangular forms, primary colors, and asymmetric balance. Although his furniture is included along with that of his contemporaries, the architects Marcel Breuer, Mies van der Rohe, and Le Corbusier, Rietveld spoke about his work in terms of fine art rather than of design. He said he made the chair out of flat boards and cut laths because he wanted to show "that a thing of beauty, i.e., a spatial object, could be made of

In addition to being chairs, these objects express complex ideas about materials, formal relationships, and presence. Left: Leonard Cave, "Boundary Chair," wood, metal, bolts. Below: Gerrit Rietveld, "Red Blue Chair" (1918/1923), beech, plywood, paint.

nothing but straight machined materials." This chair, which reads as a composition of colored planes and lines in space, calls Piet Mondrian's late abstractions to mind as much as it makes us think about seating. Rietveld's comment can be understood in two opposing ways. On the one hand, he is directing his attention to the use of a geometric vocabulary in order to construct an abstraction of a chair. He is concerned with the formal relationships allowing for an aesthetic experience. On the other hand, Rietveld is interested in demonstrating that an object of utility such as a chair can be constructed simply out of inexpensive machined materials. In juggling these contradictions, Rietveld was a precursor of contemporary furniture artists.

Context

Even earlier in the twentieth century Dada artists questioned the importance of context in determining whether a mass-produced object of utility could be apprehended as art. Marcel Duchamp, in particular, raised this question by exhibiting a number of "ready-mades," including the infamous urinal. Movements like de Stijl and the Bauhaus, sought to integrate the applied arts and the fine arts. Later, Pop artists borrowed images directly

Through performance and narrative, some furniture artists explore relationships among people, and between people and objects. Above: Scott Burton, "Urban Plaza," New York City. Right: Jon Sutter, "Under Continuous Monitor" (2000), painted wood, aluminum, concrete, plastic, found objects, 33"h.

from popular culture, sometimes restating these in art materials, such as Jasper Johns' bronze casting of a coffee can filled with his paint brushes.

Jon Sutter has made a series of furniture pieces whose faces he has filled with an assortment of measuring devices, including clocks, in the form of circular inserts. These technology centers explore the traditional grandfather clock form of a long rectangle with a more square rectangle perched on top. As he changes the relationship of scale between the two rectangular forms, we are reminded of a variety of popular cultural icons, including gasoline pumps, pay phones, and radios. Antennae suggest that these are centers capable of receiving signals from the atmosphere. With their rectangular cabinetwork carpentered out of aluminum and often bolted onto a wooden base, we wonder if these are exhibition cases meant to contain specimens for our observation. Or perhaps these sentinels are specimens themselves, with only an ironic relationship to anything else.

In the 1980s all classes of popular imagery were appropriated by painters and sculptors. Today installation and performance artists script utilitarian objects into their narratives. When these furnishings later become stand-alone objects for gallery viewing, they are recast as documentation of a past art event. Function, as it is used by some art furniture makers, demands a state of complicity between the object and its owner/user which then instigates a loosely scripted performance. A particular performance requirement is orchestrated into the object's design when the maker scores how his object will be used.

Ceremony

A Keith Crowder "Shaman Light" carries the associations of a talisman, seeming to possess some magical power created out of the combination of its imagery and presentation. Turning on the light releases a mysterious energy into the room. This ritualistic performance places the art experience in the act of use itself. The object/furniture provides the text. The light works simultaneously as light, in the actual sense, and also as an important element of the imagery, lending energy and meaning to the entire experience of the work. Crowder's larger furniture uses pre-industrial forms of joinery, such as lacing. Hemp and leather function as formal as well as connective elements. The act of using any of these pieces of furniture forces one to enter into a dialogue with

Natural imagery, elemental construction, and a sense of ritual use speak of the mysteries of life. Keith Crowder, above: "Chieftain Lounge" (1985); left: "Shaman Lights" (1986).

it. Though this furniture is entirely functional, it has a ceremonial or ritualistic aspect sparked by the associations of exotic cultures it brings to mind. References to animal and other natural forms, here integrated as structural elements such as leg and torso, continue the connection with the mysteries of life that this furniture obliges the user to enter.

Wendy Maruyama's chests and cabinets have a ceremonial air. In her earlier work, organic painted and carved elements are attached to the

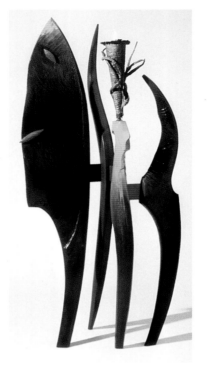

Furniture that suggests ceremonial use also invites participation in its rituals.

Wendy Maruyama, top left: "Brandy Cabinet" (1989), yellow satinwood, polychromed wood, neon, 76"h; top right: "Cone Candelabrum," collaboration with Chris Lowe (1996), polychromed and carved wood, electroplated copper, prismacolor, 77"h; above: "Ugui" (2000), wood, stone, 18"h.

surface of otherwise straightforward furniture forms. These organic forms are reminiscent of the stones and arrowheads strapped to the fetishes of Native American Indians. While they might function as drawer pulls or legs, they appear just as often to be simply appended to the surface. In recent work, these podlike shapes have become more subtle. Sometimes they become the actual form of the piece. At other times a cabinet, for instance, might read as fine furniture in its execution and lines, yet have a series of large pods carved onto or colored into the surface.

Maruyama's pods have come to signify a large body of her work. We recognize these shapes as her personal vocabulary. Her use of them to create a ceremonial context for the object they adorn is but one form they take in her work. In earlier work the color of the pods was more garish and their integration more obviously sculptural, often taking on the qualities of imagery. They seemed to have the attributes of "things." Recently, Maruyama has been adding formed copper panels as decorative surfaces. On these

she develops her imagery, adding color to the copper. Maruyama occasionally uses these personal forms in a playful way, beckoning the user to participate in her text. "Shut up and Kiss Me" is a wall cabinet holding lipsticks, a mirror, and space for other small accessories of personal adornment (see page 108). To open this small cabinet, the participant must part its "lips." Other new work integrates found objects from nature, such as branches and stones, into the lids of containers with generic interiors. Here mystery has prominence over function. Filling the interior space of one of these cabinets with stuff would detract from the charged energy of its interior emptiness.

Vocabulary and Style

As can be seen in the range of work by Maruyama, an art furniture maker's vocabulary can move away from abstraction to become imagistic, or it can remain formal and abstract. The furniture designs of Ray and Charles Eames exemplify the formal extreme. Beginning with the experimental sculptural objects cut and then bent from molded plywood splints and ending with the molded shapes of their chair seats and backs, it is easy to identify the personalization of their original source of inspiration in the work of Joan Miró and Alexander Calder. Woven fabrics designed by Ray Eames often drew from that vocabulary of biomorphic shapes. Flatten out an Eames chair seat, and it becomes a biomorph. Less widely known, the more contemporary work of Marc Newson also demonstrates a biomorphic sensibility. Newson's furniture has an anthropomorphic quality that tends to make it whimsical. His "Lockheed Lounge" evokes Airstream trailers because of the way its aluminum skin has been riveted over a large curvilinear body. The feet animate it, as if caught in a moment walking around the floor. The formal vocabulary extends, taking on the characteristics of imagery.

A number of art furniture makers have similarly adopted a vocabulary of biomorphic shapes, but each has articulated it differently. These differences personalize each body of work, making it possible to know one furniture maker's style

Some furniture artists speak eloquently through a spare and formal vocabulary. Left: Ray and Charles Eames, "LCW Lounge Chair" (1945). Below: Marc Newson, "Lockheed Lounge" (1986). (Photos courtesy: Vitra Design Museum.)

from another's. Steve Madsen, Mark Hazel, and Richard Ford Jr. all have distinctive vocabularies that include biomorphs. Biomorphic shapes first became identified with the Surrealists, of whom Miró was one, as well as Calder, peripherally. The Surrealists invented much of their vocabulary by tapping into the unconscious via automatism and autonomic writing. The resulting "free forms" appeared in their free-associative markings. The geometry of the Cubists, who had a much more calculated interest in breaking down the experience of three-dimensional space into a series of flat planes, translates most clearly into the furniture of Gerrit Rietveld.

When furniture makers appropriate fine art vocabularies, they translate them into styles. While the vocabulary of a modern art movement is formed around philosophical concerns, furniture styles that originate in the design industry are often motivated by the introduction of new technologies as well as by such socioeconomic considerations as price. The tubular steel constructions of the Bauhaus era came about as these materials were being introduced into manufacturing. A style may also be the result of fashion. A certain "look" becomes popular for a

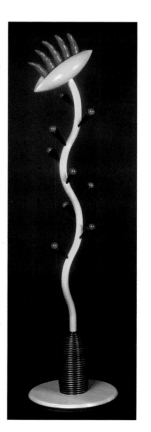

Biomorphs abound.
Left: Richard Ford,
"Dr. Freezemizer" (1999).
Above: Mark Hazel, chair (1984).
Right: Steve Madsen, "Hat Rack"
(1999).

while, later to be replaced by another. Fine art often drives fashion by lending a vocabulary. However, among fine artists the interest is usually long gone by the time a vocabulary has turned into a style.

Syntactical Shifts

Syntax in the fine arts is the way in which a vocabulary is organized. Thus an important organizing device, such as the depiction of space on a picture plane, has had many "reads" through the twentieth century alone. The Impressionists put particular emphasis upon the effects of light and atmosphere as an organizing principle. Realistic painters, no matter how farfetched their imagery, have relied upon the rules of linear perspective. Cubists organized the experience of three-dimensional space into a succession of geometric planes. Abstract artists use any of these methods, or they may choose to eliminate depth altogether in favor of a flattened figure-ground organization.

In contrast, syntax in fine furniture is a given: A chair's arms, legs, seat, and back belong in a particular order corresponding to how we sit. The same is true about syntax for beds, tables, and other traditional furniture forms. The art furniture maker may try to reinvent syntax, but this is next to impossible unless the way in which a traditional form will now function also changes. Some of Achille and Pier Giacomo Castiglioni's seats are challenging in this way, notably their "Mezzadro" and "Stella" stools, made of a tractor seat and a bicycle seat, respectively. Neither of them is stationary in the usual sense. Though designed in 1957, it was 1983 before either design was put into production.

Using a spare yet expressive vocabulary, the contemporary designer Shiro Kuramata rethought the syntactical assumptions we make about function. At times his designs challenged this tradition by restructuring an established furniture form, as in his "Laputa" double bed, long and narrow with two headboards. Instead of side by side, the sleepers must lie feet to feet, or head to head. The warmth generally associated with two people sharing a bed is here replaced by an intense feeling of alienation. This emotion, evoked through the felt distance implied by the bed's elongation, is reinforced by its cool rendering in tinted aluminum and thin silk coverlets. In other pieces, Kuramata's structural shift is strictly illusory. His oddly poetic chair "Miss Blanche" is

In art furniture familiar functions find new forms. Achille and Pier Giacomo Castiglioni, "Mezzadro" (1983).

The traditional artistic strategy of reinventing syntax is difficult to apply to furniture. Shiro Kuramata, "Miss Blanche" (1988).

constructed out of cast acrylic shapes with artificial red roses embedded in them. These semi-invisible acrylic blocks are suspended atop spindly legs of tinted aluminum pipe. The seat configuration appears to be weightless, supported on legs that look incapable of holding up much mass. This floating sensation, aided by the transparent nature of acrylic, is reemphasized by the random scatter of roses. Caught in the moment of suspension, the roses call up our associations with

Some furniture artists substitute a personal vocabulary of invented forms for traditional furniture elements. Jamie Russell, "Lucca Invicta" (1998).

Narrative elements invite, and almost require, people to see about decoding them. Below, Tommy Simpson, "Carpenter's Chair" (1991).

love and longing, reminiscent of the Tennessee Williams character Blanche, the chair's namesake.

Rather than reinventing syntax, many art furniture makers substitute a personal vocabulary of invented forms for traditional furniture forms. Thus Jamie Russell builds a table in which a carved animal skull with tusks supports a glass table-top. An outstretched frog becomes a structural element connecting another table's legs. Craig Nutt builds otherwise traditional looking tables and chairs out of vegetable parts. This type of art furniture employs wit or a hidden political message, often in the form of visual punning. When art furniture is expressive, it is usually light-hearted. Few people want to entertain their guests surrounded by furniture that is loaded and ready to challenge one's moral or political beliefs, at least not directly.

Tommy Simpson's open-ended series of natural mixed-wood chairs comprise an array of oddly juxtaposed elements, all of them functioning chair parts. Slats at the back of a Simpson chair might represent just about anything: giant paint brushes, Greek columns, flowers, heads, tools such as hammers and rulers, and so on. Some of these chairs are memory pieces. Whether it is the integration of old family photographs or other memorabilia, the effect is of a story, personal in origin. When a piece of furniture contains narrative imagery, then its use demands some acknowledgment or participation in the associations that imagery calls to mind. These chairs are functional but never without creating a hyper-conscious sense of message.

Made by Hand

In each of these cases vocabulary and expressive content are tied closely to function. It is when the piece of furniture performs that its whole meaning comes into play. Another, perhaps more subtle, opportunity for expressive content comes through decisions about the degree to which the maker allows the process of fabrication to remain in his work. The hand has always been an important presence in painting, drawing, and sculpture. What is meant by "the hand" is, in simplest terms, that the completed work looks handmade. Because a degree of roughness remains, the painting or sculpture reveals something of that decision-making process through which it has come into being. At one extreme is the work referred to as "raw." At the opposite extreme, artists whose work is described as slick, such as Salvador Dali, are considered to be less the artist and more the technician. This distinction between artfulness and technique is made in each of the fine arts, including music and creative writing. Too much craft, or "polish," is said to remove the soul from a work. It kills the art.

A brief disappearance of the hand in the 1960s and early 1970s signaled the temporary shift in aesthetic position away from the expressive and toward the strictly conceptual. Sculpture that was architectural in scale was industrially fabricated from welded steel, instead of the more traditional bronze sculpture cast from such artist-manipulated materials as wax, plaster, or clay. Tell-tale finger prints, pressure points, and tool marks translated directly into the bronze. Along with Minimal and then Conceptual sculpture came Hard Edge painting. Flat, no-brush-stroke areas of color were bound by edges created with masking tape, rather than drawn by hand. This cool line had none of the irregularities that give the drawn line a pulse, or, as furniture maker Art Carpenter puts it, "vibrato." The artist was a mind, creator of an idea that someone else might just as well have executed and often did. Craft was subverted.

Within the history of twentieth-century art, the dominance of this shift was short lived. The larger issue it reflected, of subjective versus objective, or personal versus universal, is, however, an ongoing fine-art conversation. The sculpture of Martin Puryear, beginning in the early

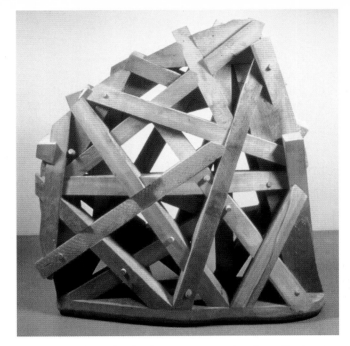

Aesthetic power can spring from the tension between the artist's sophisticated investigation of conceptual forms and evident hand craftsmanship. Martin Puryear, above: "Thicket" (1990), basswood, cypress, 67"h (courtesy McKee Gallery, New York); left: "Timber's Turn" (1987), red cedar, Douglas fir, 94"h (collection: Hirshhorn Museum and Sculpture Garden).

1970s, presents an example from within the fine art tradition of an artist attempting to merge the hand, the personal, with the conceptual. Puryear's typically organic forms are also minimal. His work represents a series of contradictions. Much of its power comes from the ways he finds to allow these oppositions to coexist within each piece. Puryear's vocabulary draws from early experiences studying woodworking in Sweden, when Scandinavian design was popular in the United States. Later, as a member of the Peace Corps, he studied the craft of West African carpenters. Puryear's work always reveals the process of its making. Though a fine craftsman, Puryear acknowledges having found ways to restrain his early leanings in this direction, for the sake of the art. His sculpture gathers aesthetic strength from his decision to keep his hand visible in his work. Our eyes enjoy a tactile going-over just as they find pleasure in the visual form and its relationship to the space around it. Our intellect reflects upon the abstraction of an idea whose sources are found in a variety of cultural histories. These forms often refer back to man-made tools, furnishings, or human dwelling places. Our emotions connect with the passionate traces remaining in something made carefully by hand.

Workmanship and Mark Making

It is a fine art point of view that the process, or performance, can be the place where the true aesthetic moment occurs. This notion is epitomized in Jackson Pollack's approach to painting, which borrows from dance and ritual. With his canvas spread out on the floor, Pollack stood at its edge or inside of it and flung his paint in calculated gestures. The painted canvas that resulted provides a record of the event. Here the focus shifts away from the audience and toward the artist or maker. The performance happens before the piece is finished rather than afterward. The "finished" piece allows the viewer some entrance into the work. He discovers remnants of the performance left behind in gestural lines and embedded debris, like cigarette butts, remaining in the painted surface.

For the process artist, the activity of making itself is creative. Although he begins with an idea in mind, it is as he builds the work that the idea actually takes shape. He is a conduit. David Pye, in his book *The Nature and Art of Workmanship*, makes a distinction between the "workmanship of risk," where the result achieved by the workman is an interpretation of the designer's plan and the "workmanship of certainty," where the design product is mass produced, each result predetermined to be the same. It is in the workmanship of risk that Pye finds the greater aesthetic value. Though a good concept is the essential first condition for either, it is workmanship that brings the design to life or not. Pye finds aesthetic merit in workmanship of risk for its own sake. Although the workman need not be the designer, the best circumstance is when the designer is also the maker. In this dual role, the craftsman is capable of an informed workmanship of risk. His decisions about how far to push his idea and when to stop keep his work lively, its surface enriched by some calculated roughness and trace tool marks that he chooses to leave behind. Diversity within execution, the result of this decision to allow some faint irregularity to

stand, enhances the work. This result of what Pye terms "the free workmanship of risk" makes a visually exciting counterpoint to the design, adding aesthetic quality. Other forms of workmanship of risk also add an interpretive element, though to various more regulated degrees.

In fine art nomenclature, marks are the idiosyncratic traces left by the artist that map his creative journey, as was true of Pollack. "Mark making" is common fine-art parlance. The difference between this activity and Pye's workmanship of risk has to do with regularity and the predictability of outcome. This is no small thing. The painter need not concern himself with any objective or measured standard for his marks, but he may. The good workman is obliged to moderate his choices in clear sight of some accepted standard. He must also keep in mind the intention of the design.

It is significant for the craftsman within our culture that, despite his great integrity, there persists a lingering association of handicrafts with poor workmanship and clumsy design. Perhaps, as Pye suggests, an aspect of this disdain is the argument made by the Arts and Crafts Movement of the nineteenth century. Pye cites passages in the writing of John Ruskin that applaud imprecise workmanship and imperfect, irregular objects as the true signs of humanity and of art. Some contemporary furniture makers, such as Drew Langsner, continue to see humanity and art in traditional crafts, enlivening familiar designs through personal variation.

When the Bauhaus reconsidered Arts and Crafts philosophy, it was indicted as anathema to its own socioeconomically motivated aesthetics. The original Bauhaus motto, "Art and craftsmanship: a new unity," was later changed to read, "Art and technology: a new unity." It is said that Bauhaus students would stay up nights sanding and polishing their designs in order to make them look machine-made. Continuing support for machine-made design over anything hand-crafted by the Design Department of the Museum of Modern Art in New York City, originally spearheaded by the architect Philip Johnson, has done a great deal to authenticate this style.

The Arts and Crafts Movement elevated rough work, claiming its imperfections and irregularities as the true signs of humanity and art. Drew Langsner, "Hearth Chair" (1999), riven oak.

The Polished Surface

Sanding to a fine finish, a prerequisite of high-end furniture, has come to be associated with good workmanship. A highly finished surface suggests that great care has gone into its creation, thus dispelling some of the bad press still surrounding handmade objects. This high polish contrasts with the marks left by the wood sculptor, resulting from his attack on the material as he finds his form. It also contrasts with the faint markings left in a surface finished by a maker dedicated to the workmanship of risk. The look some studio furniture makers achieve is often more refined than any object machined to satisfy popular standards. In a social context, we associate smoothness and refinement with material wealth. Among these studio furniture makers there is an odd juxtaposition of one set of values against another. The rectifying principle is, most likely, an aesthetic of excess. The assertion is that something handmade can be better designed and better made than something mass-produced. It can achieve the same or an even greater machined surface quality, or look. No tell-tale irregularity, roughness, or diversity need remain noticeable on the surface. Mark Kingwell, who teaches philosophy at the University of Toronto, attacked "smoothness" in a convocation address he gave at

the Nova Scotia College of Art and Design (and published in the July 2000 issue of *Harper's*). "Smoothness," he warns, "signals comfort, ease, respite from the hard or the challenging." Because "the aesthetic and the ethical are not separable," Kingwell tells us to beware of our craving for smoothness in the actions and artifices that make up the social order of the day. Smoothness can conceal societal ills.

Beyond its subliminal social messages, the aesthetic arguments in favor of achieving a highly polished surface are numerous. Smoothness is visually seductive. Sanding a piece of wood to a fine finish reveals the beautiful character of its figure just as it erases the hand of the maker. Though this attitude is argued to relate back to the purist tradition of truth to materials, it is equally significant that a polished surface, we are told, is easier to clean, therefore more functional, than one left rough. This adds to its marketability. A well sanded surface also reveals the excellent "invisible" joinery of a master craftsman. The hand is reintroduced, in a sense, but in terms of its technical prowess rather than its personal idiosyncrasy. Such a high degree of crafting erases the expressive content that results when the hand is left in the work. During the 1980s, Wendell Castle's production of historically inspired furni-

Technique taken to extremes creates a seductive smoothness that obliterates craftsmanship while paradoxically calling attention to it. Wendell Castle: "Writing Desk with Two Chairs" (1981), curly English sycamore, purpleheart, ebony inlay.

ture, highly technical, and finished to the nines, was archetypical of this approach. His workshop slogan at that time, "more is more," reflected this aesthetic of excess.

A Duchampian Gesture

When Garry Knox Bennett, in a Duchampian gesture, drove a nail into his finely finished cabinet door, he was leaving a symbolic mark. It did not destroy the finish on the piece of furniture as a whole, nor did it really represent his process. It was a calculated assault, significant because it was so out of context. This act of sabotage questioned the grounds for valuation as furniture. It was reminiscent of musical compositions by the Dada composer John Cage, during which the piano itself is systematically destroyed. Bennett increased the art value of his work by destroying some of its traditional furniture value. Metaphorically, this action addresses the nonnegotiable difference between the two traditions.

Furniture makers who leave chisel marks usually do so with great finesse, the risk of failure always at hand. Wendell Castle is so skillful with a chisel that his gouge marks are naturally precise and polished. He occasionally leaves these marks in much the same way that a draftsman may build his surface out of a series of deliberate markings. The diversity within these marks, as well as the resounding echo of the hand that made them, add to the aesthetic richness of his finished work. But when Castle uses a chain saw to create a volume, he is certain to sand away the tool marks and to refine those volumes and contours this assaultive tool has revealed.

In conversation Castle has made the connection between his work and the earlier forms of the sculptor Constantin Brancusi. Perhaps he was thinking of the elemental volumes that sit atop Brancusi's rough-hewn pedestals, a similar approach to the simplification of organic forms. However the pedestals, which Brancusi considered equally, get a lot of their power from their direct conception. The rawness of their fabrication keeps them fresh and present. Brancusi, on at least one occasion, exhibited six pedestals as finished works in their own right. It is evident from Brancusi's imagery that he also studied African art, masks, and other forms in which the tool marks, in addition to defining the form, communicate an expressive content. Raw markings fall in the domain of the fine arts. Rather than enhance or diversify a

A Duchampian gesture. Garry Knox Bennett, "Nail Cabinet" (1979), padauk, glass, nail, 74"h.

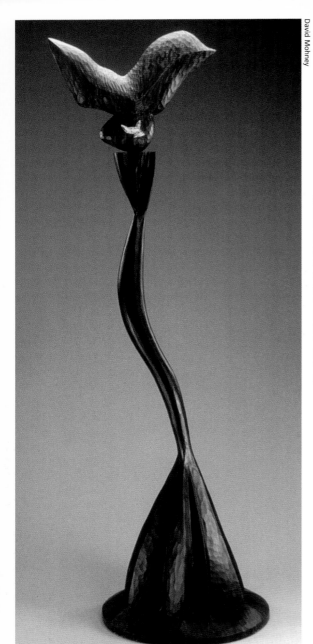

David Mohney

Some surface marks, though expressive, result automatically as artifacts of manufacture, while other markings are deliberately created in order to advance the artist's narrative.
Left: Wendell Castle, "Time and a Half" (1996), polychromed wood, 92"h.
Below: Constantin Brancusi, "Chimera" (1918), oak, 60"h.
Right: Tommy Simpson, "Snowcheeks Hill" (1995), painted basswood, 78"h.

Courtesy Philadelphia Museum of Art

surface, they may overpower it. The sculptor's markings may be intrusive and bold, taking on a life of their own.

Painterly Surfaces and Sculptural Forms

Tommy Simpson has a large body of work in which his chisel marks provide structural passageways for the painterly surface laid over them. These energetic pieces are full of color and texture that create playful narratives with a free associative feel. The deliberate nature of these markings, which seem to fall into their right place describing a movement or an area within the surface, look as if they have been incised into the wood after the large piece has been made. In other words, these are not the artifacts of its making. This is a painter's approach to surface.

Leonard Cave, on the other hand, approaches furniture making uncompromisingly out of the sculpture tradition of Brancusi and Henry Moore. Cave's pieces display the history of their making. Though function is present as a fact of the formal relationships he creates, concerns beyond that fact, such as comfort and transportability, are nonessential. Cave is most concerned with volumes and with how they communicate in space and with one another. Their reference to functional form, to the chair in particular, is abstract. In "Big Oak," Cave has carved the chair shape into a section of tree trunk, while still maintaining its monumentality. In our appreciation of this work we are reminded of the symbiotic relationship and the contrasts between the majestic tree and our own smaller form.

Cave respects the natural qualities of his material, whether stone or wood. Leaving the material much as he has found it, Cave takes his tools to the rough volumes, entering a dialogue with them. In this respect his approach comes from a long tradition of sculptors who had great respect for their material and strove to expose something they saw within it. Cave's tool marks record his dialogue with the material. Sometimes these marks work to unify the various forms making up a piece. At other times his marks are simply a record of the high-impact tools with which he works, deliberately left unaltered.

The furniture of Howard Werner contrasts with that of Leonard Cave in interesting ways. Each begins with the tree trunk, and each artist develops a vocabulary out of his personal struggle with this natural state of the wood. But the similarity ends there. The surfaces of Werner's work are rendered with a fetishistic degree of smoothness and polish. They contrast in the extreme with the original rough tree trunk, whose ghost is still present. The bark has been stripped away, exposing the natural undulations and irregularities just beneath, some of which are carved only slightly, as if to refine what nature has left unfinished. The numerous cracks in the endgrain, which are left open, have been worked into, their edges rounded and their insides smoothed. It appears as if the fallen tree has been washed and scraped clean, sanitized. Massiveness is all that remains of the untamed tree, and in place of its original textures, a gemlike quality.

The Wall Between Art and Life

Every art furniture maker must make his or her own peace between two paths that are often at odds. This carefully considered balance is always open to question. Perhaps, because it is so often precarious, art furniture will be short-lived within the studio furniture movement. It is a rocky marriage, full of compromise when most successful as furniture, representing sacrifice when it is not. The artistic importance of art furniture lies in the questions it raises and in its attempt to push against the wall that separates art from life.

Seen as a movement, art furniture has already stirred things up. Its occurrence reflects our times, which thrive upon the continual challenging of assumptions. The conflict that a piece of art furniture manifests is between two traditions, two different sets of expectations. The misgivings that

Some furniture artists conduct a meaty dialog with their materials, while others strive to rarefy their qualities. Both approaches have the power to breach the wall between art and life. Left: Leonard Cave, "Big Oak" (1999), oak. Below: Howard Werner, "Untitled" (1993), cottonwood.

art furniture seems to provoke point to the ways we have compartmentalized our lives. It is good to be reminded of this from time to time.

And what if the two traditions did merge in our lifetime? Fine furniture pays homage to its past, to its craft, valuing form and having little interest in expressive content beyond the obvious—design and status. Fine artists value idiosyncrasy, risk, and the unexpected. Ideas rank far above craft. Rather than paying homage to tradition, the point of being an artist is to question the very nature of art. Surely there is a place for this dialogue in furniture design. ■

The Next Moment in Studio Furniture

GLENN ADAMSON

Let's get
uncomfortable

A Toronto show in the summer of 2000 offered the opportunity to see furniture that is about comfort—not only aesthetically and ergonomically but conceptually. John McKinnon, "Bed"(2000), steel, fabric; "Divider" (2000), walnut, steel. Scot Laughton, "Jubejube Lamps" (2000), earthenware, electrical components.

The arts have a long tradition of resisting tradition. In most creative fields there is a relentless pursuit of the new. An endless procession of avant garde ideas consigns past ideas to the rubbish heap. In the visual arts, where the latest thing is generally the only thing, one simply cannot paint or sculpt or dance in past styles and be considered relevant as a contemporary artist. Continuity, tradition, and conservatism are not an option.

The crafts are not like this. Craftspeople respect their own past to an unusual degree—perhaps because they flirt with anachronism by their very choice of occupation. And this is as true

of the furniture field as any other. Ask a woodworker whom they most respect as a maker, and you're most likely to hear names like Esherick, Maloof, and Krenov—names you might have heard thirty years ago. More often than not, pieces of studio furniture themselves wear this reverential attitude on their sleeve. Furniture continues to be made and sold today that looks very much like the furniture that was made in 1970, 1910, and even 1750.

There is nothing wrong with this state of things, any more than there is anything wrong with a chair made in 1750. Respect for designs, makers, and ideologies that are past their prime is a large part of what makes studio work humane—what separates craft from its more grasping, desperate cousins among the arts. No one should dismiss or undervalue the continuing viability of furniture making traditions. But the conservatism of the furniture field can also have a downside, especially when tradition is taken as an acceptable substitute for the presence of a true avant garde. For any movement or community to maintain its vitality, and offer something to the world outside itself, it must continually generate new ideas. And for some time now, I would argue, studio furniture makers have not taken this objective particularly seriously, or approached it with much rigor. We have been waiting for the next meaningful moment in studio furniture to happen for at least a decade, and perhaps longer.

Today's widely acknowledged leaders, as good and relevant as their work may still be, were already the leaders in 1990. They are the generation of stylish postmodernism, the group that Edward S. Cooke Jr. dubbed the "Second Generation of Studio Furnituremakers." Many of them were trained in the 1970s, and almost all produced their defining work in the 1980s. These figures rightfully occupy the prime teaching spots in the prominent academic furniture programs, which are the breeding grounds for forward-thinking furniture. Their work makes up the bulk of studio furniture collections in the museums that are obligated to define the field. These teachers would like nothing more, I suspect, than for their students to surpass them by challenging their presuppositions about furniture making. But there are logistical barriers to such breakthroughs.

Ambitious young makers rarely enjoy the opportunity to make and sell the furniture that will point towards new ways of thinking. In a perpetually tight market the temptations of making saleable production work instead are considerable. To move forward from stasis, the field needs more residency programs like the one at Anderson Ranch, more high-level teaching opportunities, and more access to more grants that will support advanced work. Above all, it needs enlightened collectors and aggressive museum acquisition and exhibition programs.

Revolutionary Furniture?

It was with these thoughts in mind that I encountered "Comfort," one of several exhibitions that were concurrent with The Furniture Society's

2000 conference in Toronto. "Comfort" brought together a group of eight local makers and designers, who call themselves the Furniture Collective: Petra deMooy, Scott Eckert, Peter Fleming, Patty Johnson, Andrew Jones, Scot Laughton, John McKinnon, and Gordon Peteran. The Collective includes not only studio makers, but also contract designers, whose work (especially Johnson's) provides a sharp and compelling contrast to the handmade objects. Partly because of this breadth of membership, the Collective proclaims itself to be revolutionary. The intentions of the group have little to do with the received tradition of studio work, as is evident from the manifesto-like invitation they issued for "Comfort," which featured a chair ablaze with orange flames.

As it turns out, though, the show was uneven in its radicalism. The exhibition was an opportunity to think past the aesthetic, ergonomic, and procedural problems of making comfortable furniture, and instead create furniture that is about comfort. What separated the uninteresting from the exceptional was the attitude that each maker took towards this premise. The better pieces in the show did not satisfy the objective standards of utility or craftsmanship, as furniture of the 1950s and 1960s might have done; nor did they exhibit sheer stylistic invention, as was typical during the 1980s. Instead, they specifically targeted comfort: only one variable in the furniture equation.

This degree of focus distinguishes the better work in "Comfort" from the type of work that Art Carpenter has aptly called "artiture," furniture that strives to be accepted as art. This was a fundamentally rhetorical ambition—not only in the sense that "art" is infinitely elastic semantically, but also in the sense that "artiture" attempted to persuade the viewer of its art-status mainly through metaphor and stylistic exaggeration. In the 1980s, then, furniture traveled far outside its accustomed parameters in an attempt to join the ranks of painting and sculpture. The better work in "Comfort," by contrast, addresses itself exclusively to concerns that are intrinsic to furniture, but it does so with the sophistication and intelligence that one expects to find in contemporary art.

Comparing two pieces in "Comfort" will make this clearer. Consider a pair of benches by Peter Fleming and another bench, designed by Scott Eckert. The formal differences, of course, are many. Fleming's benches are massive, hewn

Having little to do with the received tradition of studio furniture, Toronto's Furniture Collective offered "Comfort" as a revolutionary presentation.

from single pieces of wood. Though well made, they do not claim our attention the way an exercise of conspicuously fine craftsmanship typically does. Eckert's piece, by contrast, is composed of finely shaped, delicately curved elements. Materials have been selected carefully, the mahogany chiming pleasantly with the caning. It is also a witty re-imagination of the bench form. In the same way that Marcel Breuer formally reinvented the chair by fashioning it from bent tubes of steel, Eckert's construction is entirely fresh. Its cantilevered form, made possible by anchors that hold the legs into the floor, yields a subtle tension between dynamism and repose.

By any traditional measure, then, Eckert's bench is the better piece of the two: it is a more eye-catching form, a more ingenious design, and more finely crafted. Yet Fleming's is the more avant garde work, and ultimately much more interesting. And no conventional woodworking standard can explain why. One must appreciate the benches at a higher level of abstraction, because they take their role as comfortable furniture not as design challenge, but as a conceptual premise. The benches are indeed for sitting—that much is clear. The absurdly anthropomorphic depressions carved into them, derived perhaps from the seats of Windsor chairs, announce that function with a deadpan directness. More particularly, the benches seem to be intended as public seating, if one can take their size and weight as an indication. And it is in this imagined context that they take on complex meaning.

Imagine them in a park: two benches with two people, both seated, as indicated by the conceit of the carved areas, in solitary isolation. Each sitter is perched on a massive timber that marks out six linear feet of personal space. The benches extend no invitation to those who would join our imaginary sitters. They accommodate the instinct for privacy more than they do the physical body—they are designed with psychology rather than ergonomics in mind. With no back and a rigidly carved, unpadded seat, the benches are not comfortable in a literal sense. But metaphorically they do offer a buffer zone, a comfort level, a place that can be irrefutably possessed. Fleming's benches reduce a complex emotion to a concise formal idea, a simplicity that is underpinned by their elemental means of construction. Compared to this kind of absorptive depth, Eckert's sleight-of-hand design seems a mere parlor trick.

If avant garde furniture makers are to develop original contributions to the arts, they must use everything proper to their medium.

Furniture's Own Concerns

Gordon Peteran's "Ark," the other powerful work in "Comfort," takes a very different path. Peteran has something complicated to say, and he says it in a complicated way. I saw several visitors to the exhibition regard it with head-shaking dismay; it was furniture they just didn't get. The piece often gets a good response anyway, because it is beyond reproach as a specimen of craftsmanship. Its quarter-sawn red oak panels tilt at unexpected angles, each one with a slightly different configuration of slanted framing elements. The interior is luxuriously upholstered in a plush red velvet. Standing on small, elegantly tapered legs, the booth is something between a Sheraton-style cabinet and a stagecoach car temporarily arrested. The thing looks like it might just leave the room under its own power—except that it is tied down to the ground by a lethal-looking tube of unknown purpose, which runs from the side of the piece to a nearby fixture.

Like Fleming's benches, "Ark" can be fully grasped only when you actually sit in it: You step in, and close the door. Immediately, you feel the pressure of people staring at you. You remember that tube and wonder what it's for. Perhaps you become short of breath. You're feeling the constriction and claustrophobia of total comfort. The desire to enter a realm of pure luxury, Peteran implies, is tantamount to a death wish. The seductive upholstered interior symbolizes the desire to escape the world, to hide, and be swallowed up. Cognates for "Ark" leap to mind: a hearse; a gas chamber; an electric chair; a torture chamber; Freud's couch.

Like Fleming, Peteran has zeroed in on the ambiguous psychology of comfort, deriving unexpected complexity from what seems the simplest of themes in furniture. This, it seems, is Peteran and Fleming's fundamental goal: to create meaning out of familiar assumptions about furniture. These pieces mark a return to furniture's own concerns, which are specific, and are meaningful because of that specificity. Despite their intellectual engagement, Peter Fleming and Gord Peteran are emphatically not sculptors. They are furniture makers, and the work they make is furniture, not sculpture.

To understand the difference between furniture and sculpture, it's helpful to look at another avant garde studio maker who bears similarities to one of the hotter young sculptors of the

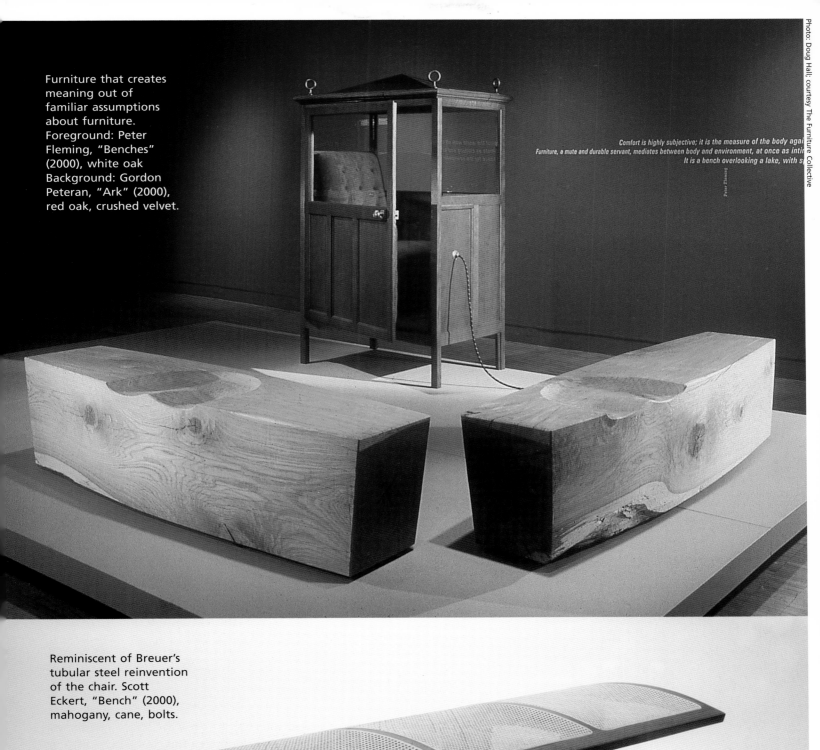

Furniture that creates meaning out of familiar assumptions about furniture.
Foreground: Peter Fleming, "Benches" (2000), white oak
Background: Gordon Peteran, "Ark" (2000), red oak, crushed velvet.

Comfort is highly subjective; it is the measure of the body aga[...]
Furniture, a mute and durable servant, mediates between body and environment, at once as inti[...]
It is a bench overlooking a lake, with s[...]

Peter Timmins

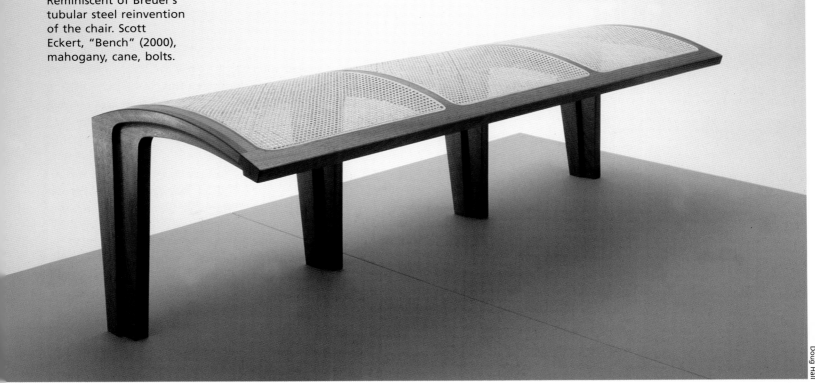

Reminiscent of Breuer's tubular steel reinvention of the chair. Scott Eckert, "Bench" (2000), mahogany, cane, bolts.

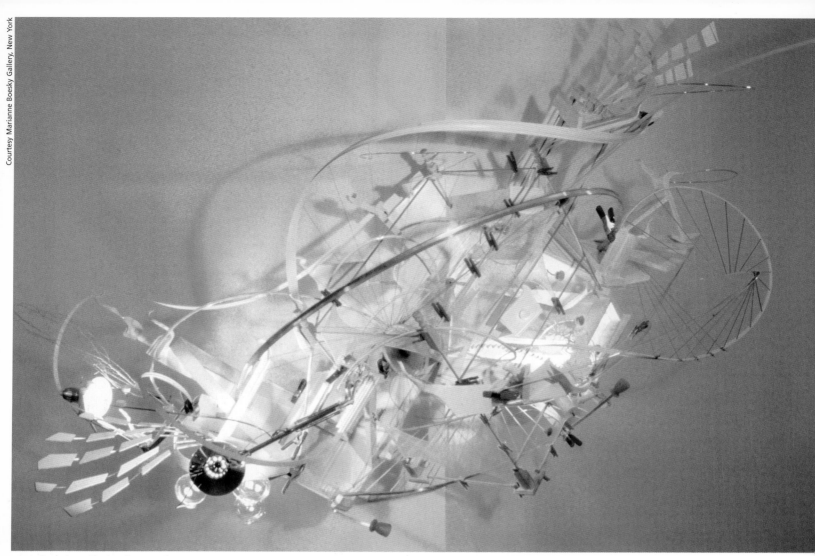

Sculpture that relies on the psychological nuances of furniture: an exploded dresser, interpenetrated with metal, string, plastic, and a pair of desk lamps. Sarah Sze, "Twice (White Dwarf)" (2000), mixed media, 211"l.

moment. The furniture maker, Atlanta's Peter Pittman, and the sculptor, Sarah Sze, both use found furniture parts, and both compose in a fractured additive style. Pittman assembles his components into tumbledown pieces of furniture that have the air of having sat in a corner for centuries, gathering to them anything that passed by. With their monochromatic paint jobs and occasional flourishes of color, his chairs seem to be viewed through the lens of accumulated memory. They draw their metaphorical power from our all-too-familiar experience of chairs as makeshift tables that gradually gather the weight of the world upon themselves.

Sze, similarly, disassembles pieces of furniture and then gracefully reassembles them in the air. Her sculptures depend on the connotations of the furniture; the work suggests frenzied violence, for example, only because the object of her destruction is a defenseless, homely dresser. By ripping it apart, she seems to violate something; by gutting a bureau, she inverts an introverted

object of containment into an extroverted sculpture. It just wouldn't be the same if she shredded a coffee table.

From Aesthetics to Concepts

So Sze relies on the psychological nuances of furniture. But this does not necessarily make her a furniture maker. That, actually, would be a more demanding role for her to occupy. Pittman's work may remind us of Sze's, and it may even communicate some of the same ideas. But it is more focused and less arbitrary than hers is. Sze's sculpture is not a dresser, but Pittman's chair is indeed a chair in every meaningful sense. And if it were not a chair, it just wouldn't be as good as it is. Despite the deconstructed look that Pittman cultivates, he actually builds in a fairly traditional fashion. The chair parts he uses mimic the usual positions of legs, stiles, crest, and seat. He is not interested in rethinking the way chairs should look, but rather in making a chair that comments upon itself as a useful form.

It's here, I think, that the current crop of furniture makers has transcended the limiting outlook of the generation that preceded them. The 1980s were taken up with a struggle for furniture's soul. On one side was functionality and fine workmanship; on the other, aesthetic freedom. The decade began, appropriately, with a great debate over Garry Knox Bennett's infamous "Nail Cabinet"—a finely made piece with a nail driven into it (see pages 12–13 and 97). In the furor that ensued, traditionalists argued that Bennett had flaunted the cardinal rule of furniture, that it should work well and look good doing it. Bennett's supporters felt that a piece of furniture could and should stand on its own as an autonomous aesthetic statement, freed from ties to traditional craft. This was the heart of the arguments over "artiture."

What is happening now, slowly but surely, is that furniture makers are bridging a second gap: from aesthetics to concepts. This move voids the importance of the previous debate over function. It makes Bennett's gesture, finally, obsolete. For when one is looking for conceptual depth, any and every device can be brought to bear, including functionality and fine craftsmanship. This is why Peteran's cabinet and Fleming's benches are at their most powerful when one sits in them, despite the fact that they are for the mind and not the body.

In this sense the new terrain of conceptual furniture is more flexible and open-ended than what preceded it. But conceptualism also demands clearer definition and more rigor than what we are accustomed to. This is the crux of the issue: if studio furniture wants to continue its contribution to the arts, it can no longer wander in the realms of pure sculptural form or whimsical, arbitrary experiment. It cannot even do what Sze does, that is, demote furniture from a medium into a subject matter. If avant garde furniture makers are to develop original contributions to the arts, they must use everything that is proper to their medium. Their tool kit will include apparently warmed-over topics such as comfort, intimacy, and domesticity. In a conceptual work, any time-honored craft technique, any historical form, is potentially relevant.

So whoever set that chair afire was only half right. Traditionalism alone may be insufficient, but it continues to be a wellspring for meaning in all studio furniture. This compact between the old and the new may not be comfortable. But the avant garde hardly ever is. ■

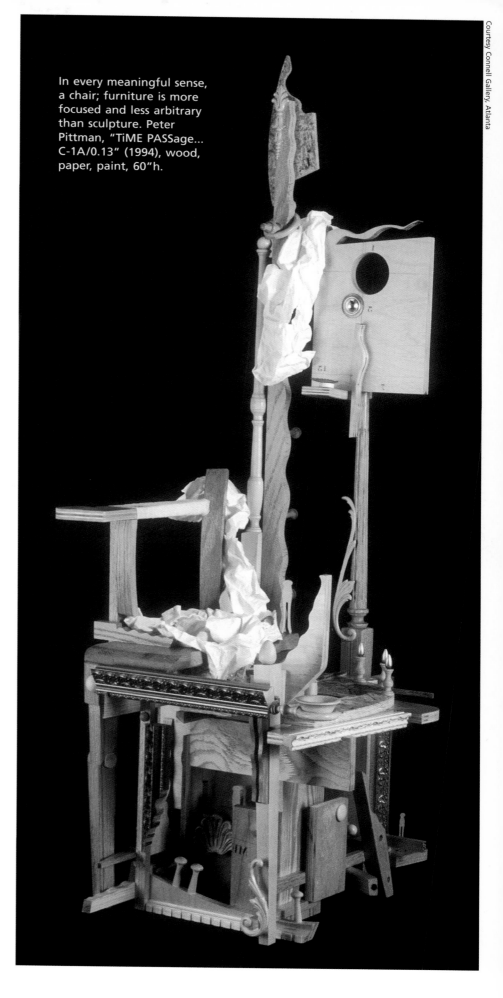

In every meaningful sense, a chair; furniture is more focused and less arbitrary than sculpture. Peter Pittman, "TiME PASSage... C-1A/0.13" (1994), wood, paper, paint, 60"h.

Furniture Gallery

PART TWO

Clifton J. Monteith
Lake Ann, MI

Moon Viewing Chair 2000
Willow and aspen
44"h × 24"w × 43"d

*Acquired in 2000 by American Craft
Museum's permanent collection in
New York City and shown in the
exhibition "Defining Craft."*

Photo: John Williams

Po Shun Leong
Winnetka, CA

Blowing in the Wind 1999

I think of this dining chair as a yacht. The back, like a sail, seems to be blown into shape by a light wind and is held steady from capsizing by the force of the thrusting double keels. Although made of only four structural elements — the seat, the back, and two legs, held together by recessed bolts and a clearly defined shape — the challenge was achieving a high level of comfort. Design guideline: Less is more.

Xanadu in a Coffee Table 1999

An encyclopedia of woods within a mahogany structure, beveled glass top
18"h × 48"dia.

The mysterious poetic fragment began:

*"In Xanadu did Kubla Khan
A stately pleasure-dome decree..."*

You look into the interior and discover architectural references to legendary places. Mazes, stairways, entrances, pyramids, ruins, bridges, obelisks, towers, domes, and temples lie.

Photos: Po Shun Leong

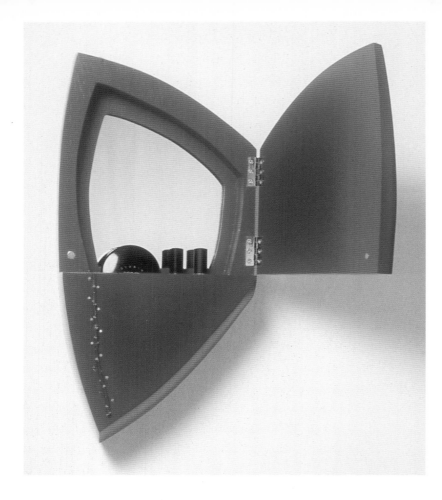

Wendy Maruyama
San Diego, CA

Shut Up and Kiss Me 1999
Polychromed wood, mixed media
15"h × 8"w × 5"d

Lipstick vanity.

Photo: Michael James

Gord Peteran
Toronto, Ontario

Beam Table 1999

Oak, bronze
30"h × 108"l × 16"d

Portrays furniture's role as a precise tool or adaptable instrument eager to engage. Both the round table surface and the rectangular vertical panel unlock and slide to any point along the nine-foot triangular beam.

Photo: Elaine Brodie

Gideon Hughes
Portland, OR

Second Base #2 in production since 1999
75-year-old galvanized tank, mahogany
76"h × 16"w × 12"d

*When I look at the rusty water tank, I can't help
but admire the zipper of rivets that someone's
skilled grandfather used to make a water tight
vessel from basically flat pieces of metal. I wonder
what that riveter would think if he knew that one
of his tanks had become a cabinet to hold the
most sensuous objects: women's lingerie. I would
love to have that conversation. The drawers lack
knobs because I want to ponder the absurdity of a
rusty tank in an elegant bedroom. The title is my
hint for how to get them open. The illogic of the
pipe work reminds me of some Dr. Seuss
contraption complete with a rope hook.*

Photo: Jon Jensen

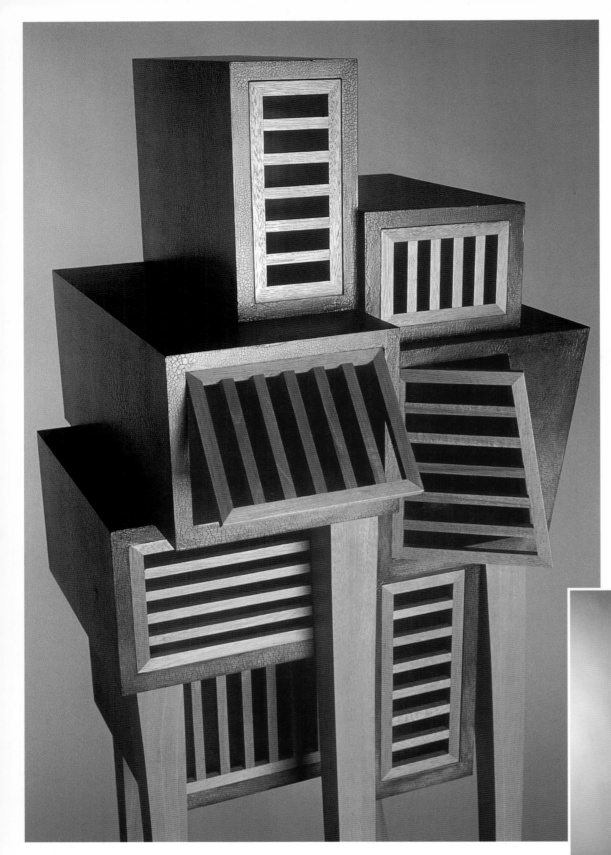

Alejandro Fernandez-Veraud
Rochester, NY

Cajas de Pajaros (Birdcages)
2000
Mahogany, acrylics
72"h × 19"w × 16"d

*The contradiction between
the old and the new creates
a rich and evocative language,
which expresses loudly the
mixed emotions of the
birdcage metaphor: the act
of love which gave freedom.
Now the birdcages are empty
but full of humanity.*

John Suttman
Albuquerque, NM

Two-Tone Gothic 2000
Steel, glass
73"h × 34"w × 14"d

*To date, my primary
medium is metal, mostly
mild steel. The exterior skin
is entirely metal. Coloration
is achieved through
patination. The fabrication
process involves cutting,
cold forming, welding,
forging, and a little
machining. I often use
wood for drawers, shelves,
and sometimes lining.*

Photo: Robert Reck

J.M. Syron and Bonnie Bishoff
Rockport, MA

Woodland Secrets 1999
Polymer clay veneers, mahogany, tiger maple
36"h × 24"w × 12"d

*The woodland forests of Pennsylvania with their ferns, trillium
flowers, and bunch berries inspired this cabinet. Inside it is lit
with halogen lights, veneered in polymer clay, and includes
shelves and drawers with hand-carved pulls.*

Photo: Dean Powell

Peter Handler
Philadelphia, PA

**Jewish Ceremonial Wedding
Chairs** 1999
Anodized aluminum, plywood frame,
fabric
39"h × 18"w × 20"d

*These are Jewish wedding chairs—
a new liturgical form. They are to be
used when the married couple is
"chaired"—lifted up in the air after
the wedding. They are structurally
overbuilt and there is a "male" chair
and a "female" chair.*

Photo: Karen Mouch

Lynette Breton
Harpswell, ME

Prayer Table 2000
Estonian bog oak, green abalone,
woolly mammoth tusk, lexan
18"h × 34"w × 19"d

The inspiration for this piece was the image of the bowl, the idea of offering and receiving, therefore the bottom of the table top nesting on the support of the base which symbolizes a gateway. Inspired by the artwork of the Pacific Northwest and the needs of my client.

Photo: Dennis Griggs

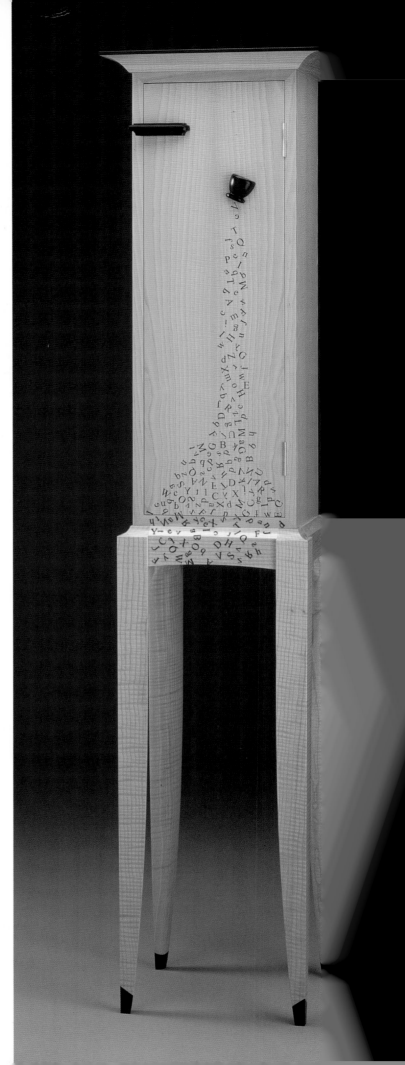

Dean Pulver
El Prado, NM

Africa #2 1999
Walnut with aniline dye,
hand carved and shaped
43"h × 23"w × 23"d

*I admire the innocence
and honesty within
primitive art and hope
to speak in a similar
voice and spirit.*

Photo: Pat Pollard

Dale Broholm
Wellesley, MA

Writer's Cabinet 2000
Curly ash, veneer and solid ebony,
dyed costello veneer, MDF
76"h × 16"w × 14"d

Lettering was laser cut.
Photo: Dean Powell

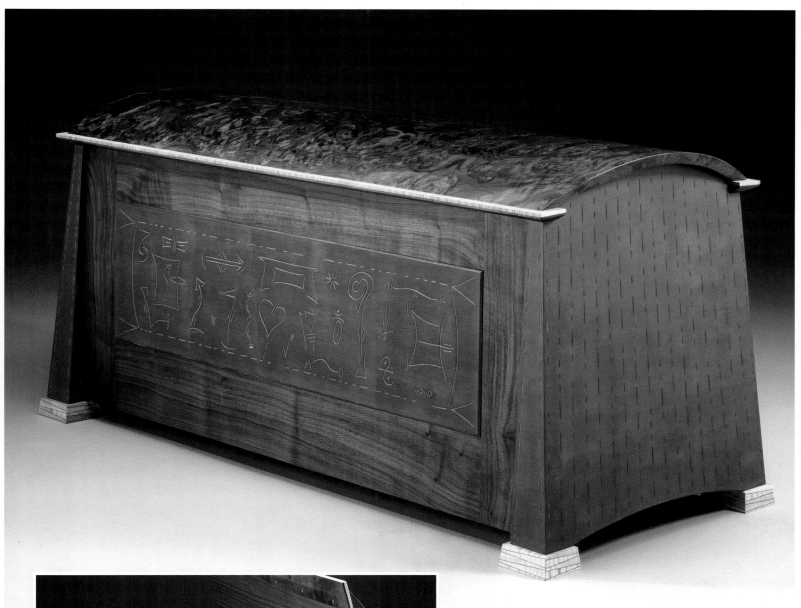

Mark Del Guidice
Norwood, MA

Blanket Chest 2000
Walnut burl, walnut, basswood, curly maple, milk
paint, varnish; 23"h × 47"w × 21"d

*Deep chest with a linen tray of curly maple. The
tapered ends are carved in Morse code: a continuous
repetition of "labor of love of labor of..." Morse code
on front panel reads "blanket chest" and "storage
place." Signature hieroglyphs on front and back panels
are intuitive carvings that I paint with milk paint.*

Photo: Dean Powell

Christoph Neander
Santa Fe, NM

Hall Table 1998
Black walnut, maple, glass
41"h × 50"w × 17"d

*How can a glass table top be
supported without the use of
four conventional legs?
Decorative joinery (tenon with
wedges) sets visual accents in
a symmetrical, balanced form.*

Photo: James Beards

Rolf Hoeg
Dartmouth, MA

Father & Son #3 1999
Mahogany, copper, milk paint
18"h × 36"–50"w ×
27"–32"d

*Coffee table/occasional table
pivots on the center (fifth)
leg creating a multi-purpose
table. The smaller table
can be stowed underneath
the larger or arranged in any
location within the
340-degree pivot range.*

Photo: Rolf Knudsen

Kim Kelzer
Freeland, WA

Chess Table 1999
Mahogany, milk paint, enameled glass mosaic
31"h × 29"w × 29"d

This game table was a collaboration between myself and glass artist Kéké Cribbs. She enameled plate glass that was then cut into tiles to form the mosaic top. We talked about color and pattern on the phone, but never saw the results until we were both finished and ready to assemble the piece.

Photo: Rob Vinnedge

Ryan Legassicke
Pickering, Ontario

One Hundred Years in the Making 1999

Ash
8'5" h × 8' w × 24" d

*Made for the show "Constructive Behavior,"
Toronto, March 2000, it was meant to sit
next to pieces of fine furniture in the gallery
and give a sense of the two extremes in
furniture making and woodworking.*

Photo: Ryan Legassicke

Andrew Ilsley
Costa Mesa, CA

Ladder Chair 1999

Oak, ash
65" h × 19" w × 32" d

Randy E. Holden
Skowhegan, ME

Adirondack-Style Buffet 2000

Yellow birch, white birch bark, curly oak veneer, Baltic birch
plywood, soapstone, beveled mirror, cut glass knobs
53"h × 60"w × 20"d

*This is a cabinet made to conceal audio components along with
a collection of more than 300 compact discs. It was commissioned
to blend with the interior of an original 1920s log cabin.*

Photo: Peter Foxwell

Rich Tannen
Honeoye Falls, NY

Outdoor Bench 1999
Red cedar shakes, white oak,
stainless steel hardware
16" h × 78" w × 19" d

Photo: Geoff Tesch

Doug Haslam
Calgary, Alberta

Stool 1998
Cherry, fabric
27" h × 19" w × 13" d

*This is the first generation of an ongoing
and evolving stool design. The seat was
created from a turned bowl form that
was split and glued together on its lip.*

Photo: Chris Thomas

Charles Radtke
Cedarburg, WI

Bedside Cabinet 1999

Mahogany, mulberry, Port Orford cedar, brass
34"h × 31"w × 15"d

*This cabinet functions at bedside and has two interior
drawers for folded shirts. The mulberry is air-dried material
that I harvested from a dead fall about five years ago.*

Photo: Doug Edmunds

Courtney Fair
Purcellville, VA

Trough #3 1999
White Oak, steel
36"h × 28"w × 54"d

*An open container made from
steam-bent white oak fastened
with forged steel pins and wooden
wedges.*

Photo: Courtney Fair

Virginia Hoffman, Sarasota, FL

Dining Table 1999
Steel, glass, brass, 30"h × 90"w × 60"d

*Perforated stainless—my favorite high-tech
material—with elegant polished brass.*

Photo: Terry Schank Photography

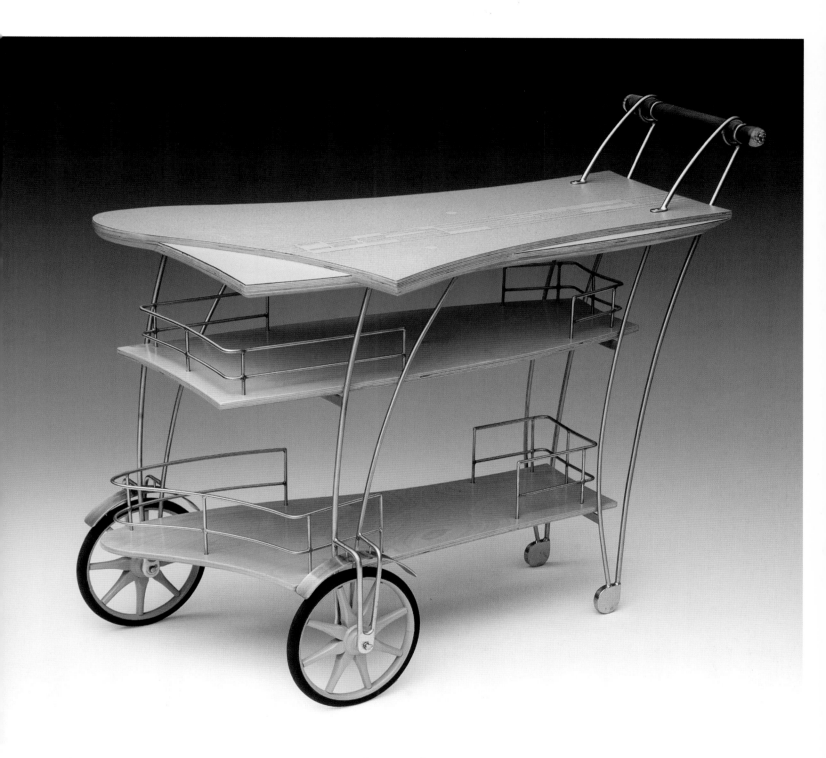

Dean L. Wilson
Oakdale, MN

Cocktail Cart 1999
Baltic birch, stainless steel, plastic laminate
34" h × 38" w × 24" d

This cart is designed for the 5 o'clock cocktail hour. Smooth shapes, cool colors, and uniquely mixed media blend together, like the perfect cocktail.

Photo: Jim Gallop

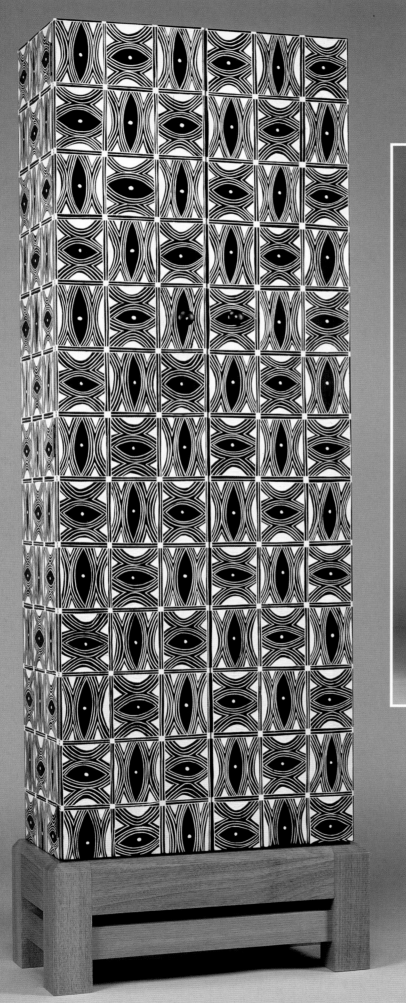

Jenna Goldberg
Asheville, NC

Tall Cabinet 1999
Carved and painted basswood, mahogany
73"h × 24"w × 12"d

*I'm interested in the way different patterns
affect each other, as in the difference between
the inside and outside of the cabinet.*

Photo: Tim Barnwell

James M. Dietz
Madison, WI

Harlequin 2000
Hard maple, dogwood
40"h × 16"w × 12"d

*Harlequin continues my exploration
into the relationship between natural
wood elements and furniture forms.
The surface patterns on this piece are
bleached—a technique I have been
developing for the past several years.*

Photo: Eric Ferguson

Danielle Bergeron
Oakville, Ontario

Elle a des Ailes 1999
Mahogany, steel
60" h × 36" w × 14" d

*The objective of the piece is to
use a minimum of components
without compromising the
strength needed in a bookcase.
The folding of a flat pattern in
sheet metal allows me to create
bookends that are integral to the
shelves. Other folds add structural
strength and serve to anchor the
shelves to the two wood ladders.
The mahogany is French polished
to achieve textural unity with the
steel. The color contrast reinforces
the function each material
performs.*

Photo: Danielle Bergeron

Jack Larimore
Philadelphia, PA

Daphne Settee 1998
Leather, curly maple, fabric
42"h × 54"h × 27"d
Photo: Carland

Timothy M. O'Neill
Basco, WI

Origami Table 1999
Ribbon-stripe mahogany, glass
17"h × 42"dia.

In addition to working with wood, I also do metal smithing. One technique used with sheet pewter is score and fold—shapes can easily be mocked up with stiff paper to create the desired form which is then transferred to sheets of metal. It has an Asian feel to it—appropriate since it was developed using folded paper (origami).

Photo: Bill Lemke

Furniture with a Sense of Place

SCOTT LANDIS

Communicating an underlying
ethical message of sustainability

Daylight is fading fast as Bruce Beeken and I return from his workshop to the overstuffed garage behind his house. We've come for his "most valuable possession," a 16-foot wood-canvas canoe that he built about twenty-five years ago. Beeken works a makeshift pulley system to lower the boat from the rafters. Gripping both gunwales, he balances the center thwart on the nape of his neck and hoists the canoe to the padded roof racks of his old Toyota. The air is cool for late July, even by Vermont standards, and in villages along the northeast shore of Lake Champlain an all-day squall has littered the ground with branches, broken trees, and power lines. It's calmer now, but two-foot swells still pile onto the rocky beach just south of Saxton Point. We decamp for the quieter waters of a stony Lewis Creek in a rig that appears to be more boat than car.

Beeken is already seated when I step gingerly off the mud bank and settle into the stern. The boat slips into a current roiled by fresh runoff and we begin our meandering descent through a sea of farmland, dotted with dark islands of hemlock. I am reminded of how, in *A Letter from the North*, E.B. White characterized the "purity of line, loveliness, symmetry" of the canoe, qualities that "arrive mysteriously whenever someone who knows and cares creates something that is fitted to do its work."

For almost 20 years, Bruce Beeken and his shop partner, Jeff Parsons, have been designing and building furniture at Shelburne Farms, a 1,400-acre environmental education center seven miles south of Burlington. Over the years, they've arrived at an approach to working wood in which core values, such as craftsmanship and proportion, are promoted by their innovative use of materials and the makers' sense of place.

When it comes to specifying wood, Beeken and Parsons are turning tradition on its head. Trees have been considered an expendable commodity for about as long as lumber has been bought and sold. But like a family that eats only what it can grow or obtain from its neighbors, Beeken and Parsons are designing furniture around the hardwood trees their local forests have

to offer. It's what foresters call "woods run," and if these craftsmen have their way, it will be foresters—not purchase orders—who determine which trees will be cut. Their challenge is to make furniture of whatever hardwood those trees yield, unfiltered and unsorted according to grade or defect. This has led them to work with short lengths and small widths and neglected furniture species such as elm, apple, black locust, and hop hornbeam, as well as woods containing the visible blemishes that might otherwise relegate them to pallet stock, chips, or cordwood. In short, what the rest of the trade considers compost is their bread and butter.

In their quest for unusual local woods, Beeken and Parsons have developed a rapport with landowners and woods workers who are improving the health, quality, and economic potential of

Jeff Parsons and Bruce Beeken and their character-laden wood enterprise.

Vermont forests. I spent several days with the two furniture makers, discussing their work and visiting some of the sources of their inspiration and material. Not usually given to small talk, Parsons chats amiably with the sawyer of a small bolter mill near the Canadian border, then stands by the carriage catching aromatic flitches of apple lumber as they peel off the blade. Beeken grins in boyish admiration when he reflects on the expertise of a logger who drops a large maple in a narrow slot between two trees, working an uphill slope in a stiff breeze. Together, the two are learning to see the forest through the eyes of loggers, foresters and ecologists, getting "deeper and deeper into the culture of the guys who get the wood," says Beeken.

The second floor of their barn workshop groans beneath 10,000 board feet of northeast hardwoods and the small kiln they've installed to dry it. Lifting the counterweighted trap door above the steep stairway to the old hayloft, Beeken and Parsons guide me past a classic wooden skiff, the building form for a small canoe, dust-caked jigs, bent parts, and assorted backwash of the trade. The dimly lit, beadboard-paneled kiln room is redolent of ancient hay and drying hardwoods. Dwarfed by stickered stacks of lumber, my guides have a story to tell about each one. The walnut was salvaged after a Burlington storm. The squirrelly apple was pruned from a nearby orchard. The beech was harvested by members of a local conservation organization.

"Here's some wood from Hurricane Floyd," Parsons says, pausing to admire a pile of locust. The trees toppled like pick-up sticks on a loamy peninsula—Locust Point—which juts out into

Lake Champlain. Commercial sawmills had no use for the wood, and the owner feared the logs would end up in the stove. In desperation, he called the county forester, who called the band-saw miller, who knew that Beeken and Parsons were on the lookout for locust.

Beeken recalls that the last time the shop bought tropical lumber, sometime in the 1980s, the butt ends of the Andaman padauk planks had been chopped with an ax. The preindustrial tool marks impressed upon the makers how far away—

The Farm Barn.

in time as well as space—they were from the natives in the Bay of Bengal who felled the trees, to say nothing of the forest. "We had no relationship with the source," Beeken says simply. Later, amid dramatic news of conflagrations in the Amazon, tropical timber boycotts, and the general confusion surrounding rainforest issues, Beeken and Parsons decided to focus strictly on local materials. "We have no shortage of unusual woods in our own backyard," Beeken says. Many, adds Parsons, could rightly be considered exotic.

Hop hornbeam is one of their favorites. Known locally as hardhack or ironwood, the species was once a popular choice for wheel hubs and wagon stakes but is virtually invisible to the furniture industry today. The stack of hornbeam in the kiln room was milled from a tree that came down alongside a trail behind the shop during the 1998 ice storm. A far cry from the wide, clear lumber that stocks the daydreams of most wood-workers, this wood is narrow, its grain wavy and heavily streaked with color, shot through with knots and other defects. Yet the hornbeam table-top that Parsons is finishing in the shop shimmers with the depth of polished granite.

TUCKED UP TO THE EASTERN SHORE OF LAKE Champlain, Shelburne Farms is a patchwork of mowed pastures and dark forests. It appears to have been shaken out like a rumpled quilt over an arcadian landscape. The property is a collection of more than thirty dairy farms and orchards that were stitched together during the last decades of the nineteenth century to make a genteel stock farm for hackney horses. Its founders, Dr. William Seward Webb and his wife, Lila, were part of the same Vanderbilt family whose fortune financed the Biltmore estate in Asheville, North Carolina. Like Biltmore, Shelburne Farms derives much of its allure from a combination of nature's largesse and the influence of Frederick Law Olmsted, an icon of American landscape design.

Olmsted developed planting lists, ordered thousands of trees, and issued detailed advice about species selections for the property. Although his involvement dwindled as work progressed, there remains compelling evidence of Olmsted's signature in the harmonious integration of the farm's residential area (the "home grounds"), permanent pastures ("park"), rotating croplands ("tillage"), and woodlands.

Famous for his edifying vistas—landscapes enriched by layers of visual elements in the foreground, middle ground, and far view—Olmsted recommended that individual trees along the roads be complemented by larger clusters of the same species, maintained a little farther back and in a more natural setting. He suggested the property's byways be "adapted with some grace to the natural landscape [superseding] the old straight and graceless public road." Today, the farm's woodland archipelago is navigated by means of gently banked gravel roads that adhere closely to its contours.

Olmsted shaped discrete outdoor spaces for utilitarian and aesthetic purposes. Beyond the formal gardens that adjoin the Webb mansion, the landscape unfolds in dramatic clumps of planted pine and spruce, which occupy the rocky hilltops. The dark masses of green foliage limn the rolling fields and suggest more space than is actually there. Everywhere you turn, prominent vistas are framed by trees—providing windows on the more expansive landscape beyond.

Charles Sprague Sargent, a contemporary of Olmsted's and director of Harvard's Botanical Garden, referred to Olmsted's plan for Shelburne Farms as "the most interesting and publicly valuable private work of the time on the American Continent." But when Beeken first approached its tree-lined meadows in the fall of 1980, the old Webb estate had fallen on hard times. Forests had gone unmanaged for half a century, roofs leaked, and exposed pine shingles were deeply weathered. The farm had narrowly survived a radical pruning of thousands of outlying acres, sold off to preserve the core, and the place was just beginning to come back to life.

Bench space had opened up in the old carpentry shop in the north wing of the Farm Barn, a castle-like, U-shaped enclosure with a stone gate, a two-acre courtyard, and a steep copper roof pierced by turrets, cupolas, and a clock tower. Beeken moved his tools into the barn and began to build custom furniture. Around the same time, a former classmate from the Boston University Program in Artisanry, Jeff Parsons, turned up at a millwork shop in Burlington. When the firm's owner approached Beeken about designing a line of furniture, it brought the two young craftsmen together. As Beeken recalls, "I had the good sense to know I had no idea how things were made in a production setting. Jeff had been doing that since school."

Beeken and Parsons formalized their partnership in 1983 and today collaborate closely on every major project the shop undertakes. Their support of good forest management and their delight in denigrated species and grades of wood coincide with the mission of the nonprofit entity that oversees the farm. This suits Marshall Webb, who manages the woodlands at Shelburne Farms from a circular aerie above the bakery in the barn's

northwest tower. A fourth-generation descendant of the original owners, Webb has the sap-stained hands of a logger. He grew up on the farm, hauling milk cans from the barn. "The whole idea," Webb says, "is to vertically integrate as much as we can." When the farm reorganized itself as a nonprofit in the 1980s, it undertook to teach the public about the full cycle of agriculture and the importance of preserving a healthy relationship with the land. "We wanted the magic of this place to rub off on as many people as possible," Webb says. "We wanted to change the bottom-line resource thinking to a long-term perspective. There was no word for it at the time, but 'sustainability' was what we had in mind." The farm's "Grass to Cheese" educational program covers everything from earthworms to pasture management to making cheddar. "We do it all in a way that we can keep doing it forever," Webb says.

He is hoping to extend the concept to trees and forests by promoting a line of Shelburne Farms furniture, designed by Beeken and Parsons, that would support the farm's commitment to sustainable resources. The Shelburne Farms management plan allows for the perpetual harvest of 10,000 to 15,000 board feet of hardwood each year, which could eventually be dedicated to furniture. To tell a fuller story, Webb muses about documenting specific logs and trees and their location on the property. "Bruce and Jeff are a critical link to the land," he says. "They use a natural resource we have in abundance and transform it into something useful, something beautiful."

Furniture helps close the circle.

Picking our way through the riffles that lie between the undercut banks of Lewis Creek, I can imagine few objects that better synthesize function, beauty, and mystery than the wood-canvas canoe, little changed since its origins in the bark boats of prehistory. The lithe cedar skeleton and canvas skin of our vessel undulate like the belly of an otter over the irregular bottom, depositing a blaze of green paint on more than a few submerged rocks.

Beeken built this beamy 16-foot canoe in the early 1970s, under the tutelage of Ed Sturgess, a reclusive outdoorsman whose traditional craftsmanship and rugged independence continue to inspire Beeken and keep him tethered to the landscape of his native New England. Beeken enjoys poking around in small streams and appears unfazed by the toll on his boat. Its fractured planks and shrinking canvas reflect an integrity that transcends its disparate parts. "Pieces of our work that I like do that, too," he says.

"Side Chairs"
(1996), white
elm, leather.

TABLES AND CABINETS OPERATE IN A NARROW emotional frequency, but chairs — not unlike canoes — communicate across a broad, visceral band. We ask more of them than we do of other woodwork. Constructed from bundles of joined sticks, both chairs and canoes are expected to withstand great loads and sudden movement while remaining portable and pleasing to the eye. At home or on the river, these artifacts promise comfort, support, and safe passage. By these unforgiving structural and aesthetic demands, wooden chairs and canoes have put many craftsmen to the test, and many have run aground.

Beeken and Parsons are probably best known for their chairs, and the makers possess an obvious fluency with the form. "Design happens in conjunction with process," Beeken says, elaborating on a prototype side chair in the shop. "We never design a piece without understanding how we're going to make it." The arms and back stretchers of the mock-up are secured with sheetrock screws to enable speedy alterations. Beeken assesses the relationship between parts of the chair in terms of "movement." He explains that the "negative" space between wooden members can be as important to the design as the legs, arms, back, and seat themselves. "Jeff has a keen eye for the movement and weight of parts," Beeken says, "and we have to be dead-on throughout, or we lose control of the form." An overwrought curve in a steambent back, a leg that tapers too quickly, a horsey shoulder, or an ill-defined joint — the errors can add up.

"We don't try to create an identity, per se," says Beeken. "It's just craftsmanship, controlling things to the extent that we can. Like sharpening a chisel properly, good design is good craftsmanship." If too many artists, architects, designers, and woodworkers approach furniture from the outside in, driven mainly by aesthetics, Beeken and Parsons converge on design from within and without, focusing on their materials, the means of construction, and the context in which their work will live. Their goal, as they like to put it, is to bring a craftsman's sensibility to a production environment.

It's one thing to build an elegant chair for a wealthy client or even a set of six custom dining chairs. It's quite another to balance comfort, durability, and aesthetics against the economics of producing several hundred chairs for an institutional venue. In 1991, Beeken and Parsons designed and orchestrated the construction of 275 cherry chairs (plus tables and study carrels) for the Cornell Library at the Vermont Law School, and in 1993 they streamlined the same design to produce 300 more chairs for the Kreitzberg Library at Norwich University. They built reading chairs for Williams College in 1994 and currently are producing 150 benches and 50 tables for the Dartmouth College ski lodge.

Beeken and Parsons recently spent half a day analyzing the relationship between a tapered leg, an end stretcher, and the side rail of a bed — a seemingly innocuous conjunction of three (almost) square parts. They clamped a basswood mock-up of the corner assembly to a sawhorse in the shop so they could evaluate the proportions from every angle. It's an intense collaboration, which Parsons describes as "figuring out how everybody gets their two cents in on a three-cent piece." Two pairs of critical eyes scrutinize every joint and chamfer, second-guess every decision. "We haven't whipped off a piece—ever," Parsons says with no apparent regret. "It changes your job," adds Beeken. "It's not me that I'm building here. I'm applying myself to an effort."

Such cautious teamwork leads to a certain reserve in their current furniture—what Parsons calls "distilled character"—as well as a lack of the whimsy that characterized some of their earlier, one-off commissions. For craftsmen who aspire to production, however, distilled seems a more complimentary epithet than whimsical. "Our furniture doesn't sell well in galleries," says Parsons, "but there are fewer stinkers."

The law school chairs provided the pair's first in-depth encounter with production, and when they engaged a Pennsylvania factory to manufacture the furniture, they did their best to eliminate guesswork. To control the critical relationships between parts, a lot of the shaping and sanding that might otherwise have been done by hand was achieved through closer tolerances in machining. Beeken and Parsons built jigs to fit the factory's mortisers and tenoners. Not satisfied with measurements, they took tracings—like gravestone rubbings—directly from machinery tables on the factory floor and designed their jigs to match.

When they revived the design two years later for the Norwich library, they put the chairs together using prefinished parts. This was their first attempt to prefinish parts in a production sequence, and it relied upon sharp tooling and excruciating attention to each operation. Parsons outlines the conventional production sequence: "Rough-out and shape the parts, do a cursory sanding, cut the joints, glue up, finish-sand. It's a great way to do...lousy work." That's because it is virtually impossible to sand cleanly to the inside corner of an assembled joint. On the Norwich chairs, they were rewarded with little or no finish-sanding after assembly, thus maintaining the crisp details they had struggled to create. "It's not just how smooth you can make it, but how close you can maintain the intended dimensions and relationships between parts," Beeken says. "Part of this is muddling through with the tools we have in the shop," adds Parsons, "but understanding the problem is the first step."

Sanders Milens

"Cornell Library Chair" (1991), cherry, leather.

Lewis Creek is one of a handful of rivers that drain the western flank of the Green Mountains. This fertile valley was once the underwater bed of Lake Vermont, created about 13,000 years ago by the retreat of the Laurentide Ice Sheet. The pro-glacial lake swelled to more than five times the area of the current Lake Champlain and was 700 feet higher, flooding all of present-day Burlington and creating shore frontage somewhere around the Ben and Jerry's ice cream plant in Waterbury, more than 20 miles inland. When the waters subsided, they deposited a calcium-rich glacial till of clay and silt, with ample nutrients to fuel the growth of the verdant forests that greeted early European explorers.

Four centuries later the towering oak, chestnut, beech, and hickory have long since departed, along with the old-growth maple and pine, which was prized by both the French and English for its precious mast timber. Writing in 1898, Vermont naturalist George P. Marsh observed that "the unparalleled facilities for internal navigation [in North America] have proved very fatal to the forests..." Any river that could float a log on the spring swell—even a tributary as small as Lewis Creek—was a likely artery for the timber that hemorrhaged from this valley. Left behind are second- and third-growth forest remnants and rich agricultural bottomland. What we see above the ground today reflects what lies beneath. The alluvial soils that were deposited at Shelburne Farms continue to foster species like basswood, white pine, and sugar maple.

TODAY VERMONT GROWS ALMOST TWICE AS MUCH wood as it did in the nineteenth century, after its ancient forests were clearcut for lumber, charcoal, and sheep pasture. But lately, real estate development pressures in combination with the widespread practice of highgrading — the successive removal of the best trees — have led to a fragmented forest landscape, a decline in forest vitality, and diminished quality of the standing timber.

Various schemes have emerged to judge sustainability — the degree to which a forest can produce high-quality trees in perpetuity, even as it protects biodiversity and wildlife, water and soil, jobs and communities. The system that has gained the greatest credibility among both environmentalists and large corporations is independent, third-party certification, as defined by the Forest Stewardship Council (FSC). Shelburne Farms is one of thirty-one landowners in the state whose forests have been FSC-certified under the auspices of Vermont Family Forests, a nonprofit conservation organization.

Shelburne Farms actively manages about 400 acres of woodlands, roughly one third of its total area. These include stands of naturally regenerating native hardwoods, softwood plantations, and a two-acre grid of sugar maples that comprise what may be the first planted sugar bush in the country. Ten to thirty acres of trees are logged each year on a cycle that precludes their harvest for another twenty years. For purposes of wildlife, wetland, or lakefront protection, almost one quarter of the farm's woods is left entirely untouched.

"We're not interested in park-like forests," says Marshall Webb, as his pickup plows to a stop in a meadow of timothy and milkweed. The adjacent forest was planted with Eastern white pine and Norway spruce during the early days of the estate. (The spruce is thought to be a legacy of the young Gifford Pinchot, first chief of the U.S. Forest Service and a lifelong advocate of scientific forest management, who advised the Webbs at Shelburne Farms.) Last year Webb supervised the removal of 35,000 board feet of softwood thinnings on this hillside. In preparation for planting in the spring, he intends to cut lanes through the dense understory of European buckthorn, a highly invasive exotic species. The trees that form the maturing overstory have been sequentially pruned in a "shelterwood" harvest to provide enough light for new seedlings, while retaining the protection of a standing forest. According to Webb, a few large maples have been left "in retirement" to come down on their own.

On an oak knoll elsewhere on the property, about 10,000 board feet of premium red oak was harvested two years ago to supply certified paneling for a new science center at Middlebury College. Stumps from the recent harvest are in evidence, as well as some from the previous cut, which took place two decades earlier. "It's chaos in a forest," Webb says. "There's so much debris on a real forest floor. But you've got these strong trees coming up. We'll have just as big red oak in twenty years as we had two years ago." Overhead, the canopy of oak branches and leaves has almost entirely closed already.

Certification validates what Webb has been doing at Shelburne Farms since he went to work in the woods in the 1960s. It helps tell the story of the farm's investment in good management even as it invites independent foresters and ecologists to critique forestry practices and suggest improvements. The largest obstacles to the property's successful restoration reflect concerns that preoccupy forest managers throughout the region: how to control invasive exotics like buckthorn; how to balance ecologists' preference for native flora with the area's long history of nonnative species; how to contain the deer population; and how to develop profitable markets for the variety of tree species that inhabit a natural forest.

Sustainability remains a theoretical construct. Forest productivity decreases when nutrients are removed, and after several heavy harvests, timber yields may be expected to decline. As environmental oracle Paul Hawken writes in *The Ecology of Commerce*, "Habitats can endure over millennia, but it's practically impossible to calculate the sustainability of...actual forests." Hawken, who is an honorary board member and advisor to Shelburne Farms, concludes that the concept of sustainability may help to reverse the "perverse incentives" that have long governed the exploitation of forest resources. "Markets are superb at setting prices," he notes, "but incapable of recognizing costs."

Mining timber is always cheaper, in the short term, than harvesting it. No matter how you define the task, sustainable forest management requires an up-front investment. It costs money to build good skid trails, install water bars that control runoff and reduce erosion, train qualified loggers, preserve wildlife habitat, and produce generation after generation of high-quality trees. The furniture industry is the highest-paying customer for Vermont hardwoods, but it offers no

Sustainability remains a theoretical construct.

premium for certified wood. Worse, manufacturers are really interested in only a fraction of the wood that grows in the forest. According to a recent study by the Vermont Department of Forests, Parks, and Recreation, slightly more than one third of the lumber milled from sugar maple sawlogs—the most desirable hardwood species in the state—falls into one of the top three grades. The remaining two thirds of every log is relegated to relatively low-value products, such as flooring, pallets, railroad ties, or firewood, which return far less profit to landowners. Of course, this statistic does not account for the huge volume of lesser-grade wood to be found in tree tops and limbs; diseased, injured, and small-diameter trees; or undesirable species that have little or no market at all.

Lower-grade timber is abundant in most forests and its harvest can improve overall forest vitality and invigorate genetic stock. By fostering new and better markets for these materials, Beeken and Parsons can help underwrite the real costs of forest stewardship. "I love a nice, consistent, straight- or quarter-grained wood," Beeken says. "It's pure. It's simple." But he and Parsons have committed themselves — philosophically, aesthetically, technically, and as a business — to using as much of every tree as possible. "Our focus is on character wood," Parsons says. "How to use it efficiently, what its potential markets are. Knots, discoloration — they're what give these pieces their flavor."

Commercial hardwood mills make their money by sawing for "grade." The sawyer typically works a log from the outside in, flipping it 90 degrees as each slab is removed. Rip, flip, rip, flip, until he reaches the knotty heart. Boards are sorted according to grade and dispatched to different markets, with the heartwood "boxed" in cants for pallet stock or ties. This procedure generates a high percentage of top-grade lumber, along with a lot of sawdust, wood waste, and no contiguous boards that a furniture maker might use to achieve complementary grain patterns or harmonious coloration. What's more, commercial mills can't handle a log under 8 feet in length and 8 inches in diameter, and they're loathe to cut lumber in the heavier thicknesses required for chair parts and table legs. Species such as hornbeam and apple rarely make it onto the saw carriage.

Beeken and Parsons prefer to maximize yield, not grade, which usually means sawing a log straight through from one edge to the other, a "through-and-through" cut. They also like to employ "green dimensioning," milling a log as closely as possible to the final sizes of the parts they require. They can thus use shorter lengths and more of each log. "Even the most spectacular tree has a heartwood full of knots," Beeken says. To relieve the unstable pressures found around the pith, Beeken and Parsons aim to slice most logs directly through the center.

Opening a log is only half the battle. When they get the lumber home, they've got to dry it without excessive splitting or warping. With

Red elm, beech, hickory, basswood, butternut, white birch, curly cherry, and white oak: row upon row of live-edged lumber, flitch-sawn, end-coated, and painstakingly stickered and stacked as it came off each log.

a 1997 grant they received from the State of Vermont, Beeken and Parsons bought a low-temperature kiln to experiment with drying local exotics. They've since dried about 10,000 board feet of lumber and, in the process, developed kiln schedules best suited to the challenging woods they use. "We're able to have very intimate control over the manner in which our wood dries," Beeken explains. "Wood that's too dry is difficult to machine, which is very important with character wood. It's tough to control. Without the kiln, we wouldn't be building with woods like hornbeam."

"A different currency"—elm harvested by a storm.

The morning after our paddle on Lewis Creek, Beeken and I arrive at the shop to find Parsons on the phone with a local tree service. A large elm came down on a lakeside home during yesterday's blow and it is theirs for the taking. "I hate to turn down elm," Parsons says, covering the receiver with his hand. Lofty piles of lumber threaten to block the windows in the kiln room upstairs, and they've put a moratorium on new acquisitions. Still, they waffle. "We love this wood," says Beeken. "When it becomes available, we make every effort to get our hands on it."

When we arrive at the house, four arborists are employing a block and tackle and several chainsaws to extricate the fallen elm from the roof and a canvas porch awning. Where the elm stood yesterday—the only shade tree between the house and a panoramic view of the lake—is a gaping dirt crater ripped in the lawn by the upended root ball. Beeken commiserates with the owner, who seems disappointed that there's no cash in the deal, but she accepts Beeken's proposal to pay for transportation.

Behind the wheel, Beeken runs the numbers. "The way I see it," he says, "we just bought a tree for fifty or seventy-five bucks." The logs might yield 400 board feet of lumber of uncertain value. "By the time it's dry, is it worth two bucks a foot? Is it worth three?" Back at the shop Parsons puts the value much higher. In any case, "I wouldn't want to make a career out of chasing fallen trees," Beeken says. "This one is elm, and we can't go out and buy it. For us it's a different currency, being able to offer something special that's connected with where we work and live."

DIRECTLY BELOW THE KILN ROOM, A LARGE gallery of windows gives farm visitors a glimpse of the craftsmen at their benches. Though neither Beeken nor Parsons shrinks from publicity, there's no sign over the door and they have never had a business card. In fact, a little obscurity helps to reduce distractions by culling their clientele. Soon, however, Beeken and Parsons will have fine-tuned their designs and worked through the glitches attending wood procurement, production, and finishing. At that point, they will begin chumming the waters for customers as they never have before.

"There are two things motivating us," says Parsons. "The first is economic, in that our ability to earn a living is based on the number of things we can build in our shop. The second is to seek some benefit to landowners, forests, and the ecology of the region. Those things won't become real unless we achieve a scale that will make a difference..." To that end, they are seeking a production facility in the region to manufacture their furniture. "There's nothing really new about using character wood," Parsons says, citing the work of contemporary masters like James Krenov and John Makepeace and period furniture embellished with gaudy burls. What Beeken and Parsons can add resides mainly in their ability to dry and machine such difficult woods and steer them through a factory.

To prepare themselves to meet the market, Beeken and Parsons organized a series of consumer focus groups, in partnership with Shelburne Farms. They watched intently through a two-way mirror as a moderator quizzed groups of eight or ten panelists about their reactions to samples of raw lumber and three small tables Beeken and Parsons built from clear, lightly marked, and heavily character-marked maple. Through these encounters, Beeken and Parsons hoped to understand public attitudes toward their innovative use of wood so that they might position their furniture to receive the best possible reception in the marketplace.

Worm holes, sap pockets, and knots elicited a variety of responses. Some focus-group participants (mainly men) worried about structural integrity ("I just don't trust the legs"); others (mainly women) voiced concerns about bugs and dust. But when the furniture was attached to a wholesome story, it invariably drew a warm response. The thoughtfully chiseled verbiage that drew the most enthusiasm was: "This wood was carefully logged from a hillside forest on a farm in northern Vermont and then crafted into tables by local furniture makers," and "The wood in these tables is evidence of the random workings of nature. The rhythm, texture, and marks in the wood tell a story of the life of the tree..." Predictably, adjectives like "hand-crafted" and "homemade" drew positive responses, while defensive phrases ("The knots, shadings, and pockets found in this wood should not be regarded as defects") were rejected as disclaimers. Universally, participants appreciated specific information about the products and the wood species but resented any effort to mold their own aesthetic judgment. As one Framingham woman put it, "The table speaks for itself—you don't have to address [the design]."

Digesting this exchange between forkfuls of dinner, Beeken and Parsons were stunned by the public's apparent ignorance about wood. Few panelists could identify more than one or two species with any certainty. And the makers were chagrined at the posturing that men exhibit in groups. "It's nothing to brag about," says Parsons. During the very first session several men became skeptical about the term "wood prod-

ucts," which they associated with reconstituted or simulated materials like chipboard or photo-veneered laminates. Skepticism turned to jaded indignation when they suspected their knowledge was being tested. Running his fingers over a smoothly sanded maple surface, one man jabbed the air authoritatively with his forefinger and pronounced, "Real wood doesn't feel like that!" After minutely examining a tabletop heavily laced with wormholes and spalting, another inquired, "How did they do this?" Presuming to solve the mystery, someone else declared that a fine black pen must have been used to simulate the characteristic thin, dark line that surrounded the spalted patches. Henceforth, Beeken and Parsons referred to spalted wood as "BiC-teria."

The focus groups were followed by six or seven face-to-face surveys, including ones conducted in Albany, New York, in downtown Boston, and at the Sandwich Fair in rural New Hampshire, where chairs and character wood were wedged between oxen and draft horses. Perhaps the clearest message gleaned from all of this public exposure was that design and function come first. Other details, such as the character of the wood, its origins, and its degree of sustainability, are subordinate layers of information that tend to reinforce a person's understanding of a piece of furniture. "Design is a powerful language. It has approximately twice the weight of price," says Beeken. "It communicates lots of different things about peoples' relationship to the material world, to themselves. It has the ability to promote the usage of this material. But I don't think one person—not even the most adamant, dyed-in-the-wool tree-hugger—will buy our chair if it's uncomfortable. Nor should they." Adds Parsons, "It's all a lot of hocus pocus until we're actually talking to people who have spent money for this stuff."

Like their materials, some of their best customers are found close to home. In honor of the state's bicentennial celebration in 1991, Beeken and Parsons were among twenty-five Vermont craftspeople invited to design an object inspired by an older example housed in the collection of the Shelburne Museum. (Built next door to Shelburne Farms, the museum property is among several parcels of land that were alienated a century ago from the original Webb estate.) The nineteenth-century country chair that animated their

"Our focus is on character wood," Parsons says. Above are details of the three tables put before focus groups to gauge reactions to clear, lightly marked, and heavily character-marked maple.

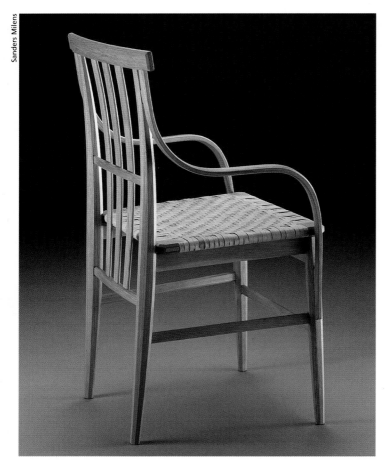

"Bicentennial Chair" (1991), made from the wood of a small diameter hickory, thinned to make room for a more promising maple.

design was, in Beeken's words, "slightly crude, a bit awkward, and ill-proportioned...but it had endless character." Built in rural Cavendish, the chair possessed a quality that Beeken says "few of us accomplished guys ever achieve." They took a stab at it but in the process, he admits, "boiled a lot of the character out." They arrived at a sinewy hickory armchair with tapered octagonal legs, a woven bark seat, and fluid, steambent arms and back. The wood came from a small-diameter tree at Shelburne Farms, thinned to make room for a more promising maple.

Over the years, the pair's designs have become ever more spare and more cohesive. It is tempting to infer a lineage from popular styles, such as Arts and Crafts, Shaker, or Japanese, renown for clean lines and purposeful detail. Though Beeken and Parsons are well aware of these decorative-art motifs, their work is not so neatly pigeonholed. Heavily shaped by a native syntax, their design vocabulary is also influenced by the exigencies of production and the complexity of their material. They find that intricate or delicate shapes and fussy details compete with lively grain,

color, and erratic features of character wood. Their maturing aesthetic owes a good deal to the Vermont landscape and its abundant reservoir of furniture, tools, and architecture found on old farmsteads. These design models include country tables and chairs, farm implements, and, yes, wood-canvas canoes.

A few years ago, Beeken and Parsons plumbed this reservoir to design a group of occasional seats for the Pleissner Gallery at the Shelburne Museum. Ogden M. Pleissner was an early twentieth-century painter who worked in the realist styles of Winslow Homer and the Hudson River School. He was best known for his distilled portraits of outdoor life. A replica of Pleissner's studio is installed at the Shelburne Museum, which houses a large collection of his paintings, along with the artist's walking sticks and bamboo fly rods. Beeken and Parsons interpreted Pleissner's work in an embracing, open-armed design that is somewhat wider than a chair, somewhat narrower than a loveseat. They wanted the benches to fit the scale of the gallery, and they were mindful of the public's various needs: that of a mother with a child, a tourist or a student toting a backpack. Reviving central elements of their bicentennial chair, these pieces were also made of steambent hickory from Shelburne Farms, with tapered, octagonal legs and a ribcage of bent slats sprung around a horizontal lumbar rail. The chair's low-profile seat is padded with sheepskin fleece and covered with two layers of cowhide.

"Scale is so damned elusive," Beeken says, "and the simpler the piece is, the more critical the issue becomes." Furniture that looks heavy in a private residence might be ideal for a public setting. Conversely, an object that appears well proportioned in the shop can be dwarfed by institutional surroundings or heavy architectural features. "When we view the success of a chair, or any piece of furniture, we think of it in context," says Beeken. "We don't always nail it, but we certainly try."

In their latest challenge, Beeken and Parsons are designing for a more extensive context. They are making sketches and prototypes for roughly 300 different pieces of furniture in seven basic designs—including tables, chairs, beds, desks, and wardrobes—that will occupy a new residential environmental education facility at Shelburne Farms. The center will be installed in the 40-by-

200-foot, two-story Old Dairy Barn, built in 1891. Meeting rooms will occupy the former ground-floor paddocks, dormitories the old hayloft. It is the vision of Paul Hawken and the "green team" advising the project that the very fabric of the restored structure will tell a story of wood, trees, and sustainable forest management. All of the lumber—from two-by-four partitions to wainscoting, doors, window trim, flooring, and furniture—will be harvested from Shelburne Farms' certified forests.

According to Beeken, Hawken described their goal this way: "When people come into their room, I want them to ask: 'Can I live like this?'" Beeken and Parsons hope the answers will be informed by furniture that's comfortable and refined yet spare, built of homegrown woods that reflect the full spectrum of the material's natural character. For Marshall Webb, the center is linked to the fulfillment of the farm's environmental mission. The furniture helps close the circle, enabling the farm to support its management activities by selling its own wood products. "If all goes well with Bruce's and Jeff's project," he says, visitors to the center will be able to "buy the bed they're sleeping in, the desk they're writing at, and the chair they're sitting in."

Standing in the cavernous hayloft of the decrepit barn, it's hard to imagine a residential conference facility, much less one outfitted with wall-to-wall furniture by Beeken and Parsons. But amid the old stalls below, the project is taking shape. Three years of sawing have yielded row upon row of live-edged lumber, flitch-sawn, end-coated, and painstakingly stickered and stacked as it came off each log. Red elm, beech, hickory, basswood, butternut, white birch, curly cherry, and white oak—there's a cache here that any woodworker would covet. Beeken demurs, "I don't consider this money in the bank. I look at it as a library." This year's sawing schedule, he points out with pride, was taken directly off their drawing board. The Old Dairy Barn project could easily furnish a career's worth of custom projects, if that were all they wanted. But for Beeken and Parsons, it represents the first time that a major project will be expected to work not only for itself but as a springboard for future, ongoing production. "It's a matter of balance," Parsons says, "a recognition of the role that economics plays in resource management."

"Pleissner Gallery Chair" (1996),
hickory, sheepskin fleece, cowhide.

I've returned to Shelburne with the dawn, in time to watch the first rays of sun glaze the copper roof of the Farm Barn. A ruffed grouse thrums on the woodland trail behind the shop. Underfoot are fresh deer tracks, fox scat, and wild turkey prints stamped in the mud. Mist lingers in the meadow hollows. On the stippled surface of Lake Champlain, a light wind rises from the south, while, in the far view, the Adirondacks slumber in variegated shades of purple and green.

Much can be gained by careful observation and living deeply, if not widely. By setting down roots in a place and immersing oneself in its community of people, trees, and waterways, one may eventually come to know it. Rare though such an achievement may be, rarer still is the ability to translate that intimate knowledge of place into a palpable object, an enduring piece of the material world. ■

Thinking Furniture Making

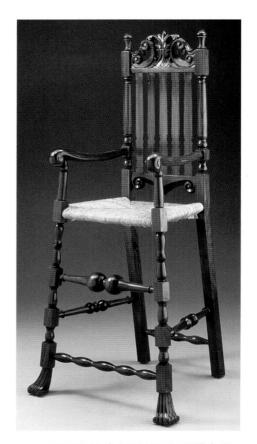

ORIGINALITY I'm not sure how it was that I came to be a maker of traditional looking furniture. It wasn't the type of furniture I was brought up with, or the type of furniture I was taught to admire. Neither did I grow up with any tradition of craftsmanship. Ideas, not handiwork, were prized in my family. So I guess my involvement with furniture making is a form of rebellion rather than the carrying on of any tradition.

Perhaps because period furniture is so foreign to me, it is interesting. I don't see tired, outdated designs but rather new, even contemporary images. I see irrational exuberance. My banister back high chair (top right), taken from seventeenth-century chair designs, can be made with a great deal of freedom and speed. The crest rail carving is bold and created by large gouges taking heavy cuts. The turnings use repetitive elements and need to be similar, not identical, to produce the desired effect.

In contrast, a Federal-style work table (bottom right), typical of furniture made a century later, is all about precision and control. These turnings must be identical to align with the case. Lines are crisp and veneered surfaces are taut. There is a cerebral aspect to the making. It is easy to see control, harder to see joy, in Federal furniture.

The question is often asked, are these pieces (and the one on page 40) mine or do they belong to an earlier era. For me, they are very much my own. The high chair combines elements from many banister-back arm chairs I've admired, but they're transposed onto the form of a child's high chair, so the robust turned legs become long and spindly, and the crest rail carving—the ceremonial crown—is reduced to an ornate, pointy top. The scale of this traditional and somewhat pompous chair form has been altered in the same way that a child has an altered view of grown ups. When seen from below, they appear to have long legs and small heads.

In the case of the work table, I was amused to recreate the obligatory hanging fabric bag in quilted maple, relying on the curly grain of the wood to resemble the traditional gathered satin fabric. It is a furniture maker's joke, but for me it is required comic relief from the serious and exacting nature of its construction.

When I think about what it takes for me to feel that the furniture I make is original, the answer seems to be: not much. It can be as simple as a pun or a juxtaposition. It can be a recombining of traditional elements in a slightly different way. Traditional furniture forms also offer an opportunity to demonstrate a very high level of technical proficiency and craftsmanship, often in techniques that are not commonly seen. On that very basic level, just the making of a piece of furniture and the demonstration of that competence can be enough to make it one's own.

— *Miguel Gomez-Ibañez*

RARE WOODS Much of my work depends on my fascination with rare woods from all over the world, small stashes that I may see only once in a lifetime. Often these timbers come with a

Miguel Gomez-Ibañez, top: "High Chair" (2000), walnut, rush; "Work Table" (1999), mahogany, birdseye maple, crotch mahogany veneer.

story. The coffee table pictured (at right) combines a beautiful plank of English brown oak with the nearly black English bog oak, excavated near the place where my client's family originated. But rare things sometimes come with surprises too. The bog oak, after 6,000 years under water, doesn't work like normal wood. Some of its inter-cell adhesion is gone, and almost every cut, even with the sharpest tools, yields a little chip or other imperfection. So this is a coffee table made of many tiny repairs and recoveries. Even a simple piece like this, seeming to express little beyond a certain attitude toward materials, speaks in the end about the kind of labor called into play by those materials. I want the care and patience of my work to be implicit in each piece I make.

— *Loy D. Martin*

SINCERITY

No matter how many lifetimes people may argue that we have, I am consumed by my commitment to this one. I am always asking myself the big questions. How does my work reflect my values? Who benefits from the work that I do? Where do I think that I have the most to contribute? Am I making the best use of my time? I have a driving need to stay in touch with why I do the things that I do.

Superficial and seductive, cleverness has found a place in the arts, but I want nothing to do with it. Cleverness builds off the cultural language of its time. It involves some easy to recognize twist or turn of the familiar. Cleverness comes from a place just enough below the surface to surprise and amuse us. We get it! What could be more reassuring or make us feel more safe in a world that has moved far beyond an easy reach? Cleverness is a way to please and to be liked and to avoid sincerity.

It took many years before I recognized a meaningful personal connection with what I produced. Few people want to deal with sincerity these days. Has its time past? Or, is there some new standard for determining this? Sincerity is messy. It can be a cause for embarrassment. It is vulnerable. It is reflective. It is rigorous. But sincerity is tied to meaningfulness, and life is messy. Again, I am questioning the sincerity of the work I do in my studio. Have I managed to resist the temptation to be clever? How must my new work reflect the recent changes in my thinking?

—*Kathran Siegel*

THE FUTURE

There's a lot of interest in traditional furniture now, particularly here in New Hampshire. And the contemporary work that's being done now or will be done in the next fifteen or twenty years will assume more importance because it'll become traditional, like, for instance, Hepplewhite stuff is now. I'm always pleading for more understanding of form, rather than just making the functional period-style cabinet or chairs. But I feel like a voice yelling in the woods with nobody else around. It may be that makers are becoming more interested in fundamental questions of form. It depends on who can hone in on a dialogue that would develop more understanding of it.

As the generations come along, I think there will always be an interest in what we call traditional furniture, but I see that changing. It will have to do with customers commissioning things. I'm not suggesting that customers lead the field—I don't think that would be a good idea—but they've got to see some examples and say they want something more like that. Seeing it in galleries, at shows, and in print, people will pick up on it.

In a way, there's too much functional furniture—I don't quite mean that—I don't like *non*-functional furniture. But it needs to go beyond being functional. Most of the time I tell myself that my work does not relate well to other furniture makers, and that's deliberate. I'm trying to come up with new forms that serve familiar functions. How good they are is another question, but at least they express things differently. So another forty or seventy years, you wait. Things will change.

— *Jere Osgood*

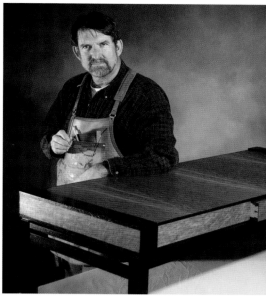

Loy Martin, "Coffee Table" (2000), English brown oak, English bog oak.

Kathran Siegel, "Table/Chair Set with Work Gloves" (2000), maple, glass mosaic inlay, acrylic, graphite, prismacolor pencils.

Jere Osgood.

CONTRIBUTORS

Glenn Adamson ("The Next Moment in Studio Furniture," page 100) is curator at the Chipstone Foundation, a private organization in Milwaukee that promotes scholarship in the decorative arts. In that capacity he teaches at the University of Wisconsin at Madison and prepares exhibitions at the Milwaukee Art Museum. He also writes for various publication, including *American Craft, Woodwork,* and *Turning Points.*

Jonathan Binzen ("Fitting In," page 61) is a writer, editor and photographer in New Milford, Connecticut. Formerly senior editor at *Fine Woodworking* magazine, he was also an editor with *Home Furniture* magazine from its launch in 1994 to its landing three years later. He specializes in furniture, interiors, and architecture and is currently editing a history of the furniture of the Arts and Crafts Movement.

Deborah Fillion (art director) is a partner of Image & Word, a print packager in Montpelier, Vermont. A former art director of *Fine Woodworking* and *Fine Homebuilding* magazines, she has been designing and producing books and magazines on crafts, gardening, home-building, and American cultural history for more than twenty years.

Gerrit Gollner ("More Beauty and More Deep Wonder," page 52) is a visual artist, woodworker, and student of philosophy living in Vermont.

Miguel Gomez-Ibañez ("Understanding Tradition," page 42) is an architect-turned-furniture-maker who has been a contributing author to several journals and magazines. He works in an elegant industrial loft overlooking Boston harbor with Fort Point Cabinetmakers, a twenty-year-old cooperative studio of independent woodworkers. He is currently working on a series of pieces that integrate original paintings into historical furniture forms.

John Kelsey (coeditor) is a journalist, furniture maker, and the publisher of Cambium Press, which specializes in books on woodworking and furniture design. A graduate of the School for American Craftsmen at RIT, Kelsey was editor of *Fine Woodworking* magazine throughout its black-and-white years, 1976–1984. He has written more than a dozen books on woodworking and other craft subjects.

Mark Kingwell ("More Beauty and More Deep Wonder," page 52) is Associate Professor of Philosophy and a Senior Fellow of Massey College at the University of Toronto. He is the author of four books in political and cultural theory and writes regularly for various publications, including the *Utne Reader, New York Times Magazine, Adbusters,* and *Harper's,* where he is a contributing editor. His new book, *The World We Want,* is published by Rowman & Littlefield.

Scott Landis ("Furniture with a Sense of Place," page 128) has pursued an elusive sense of place in various locations, from northern Ontario to his current home in southern Maine. He is the author of *The Workbench Book* and *The Workshop Book,* and has published dozens of essays and articles related to woodworking traditions and sustainable forestry. He produced the traveling exhibition and catalog, *Conservation by Design,* and directs the GreenWood training project in Central America.

Loy D. Martin ("Decoding Studio Furniture," page 8) earned a Ph.D. in English literature from the University of Virginia in 1973. He taught in the English departments of the University of Michigan, Stanford University, and the University of Chicago before leaving his academic career in 1982 to design and make studio furniture full time in Palo Alto, CA. Since then, he has written for the furniture field, and his furniture has

been pictured in various publications and shown in a number of West Coast galleries.

Rick Mastelli (coeditor) is a craft editor, photographer, videographer, and sometime woodworker. He was associate editor of *Fine Woodworking,* editor of *American Woodturner,* and founding editor of *Furniture Matters* (The Furniture Society's newsletter). As a partner of Image & Word, he has produced or contributed to a number of books and videos on craft, gardening, homebuilding, and American cultural history.

Jere Osgood ("A Meditation on the Desk," page 72) has been a leading force in studio furniture, both as a maker and a teacher, for more than forty years. He has taught at various schools, including the Craft Students League, Philadelphia College of Art, the School of American Craftsmen, and Boston University's Program in Artisanry, for which he was also acting director. His work is included in such major collections as the Boston Museum of Fine Arts, the American Craft Museum, and the Renwick Gallery of the Smithsonian Institution. He is currently dividing his time between another shell desk and committee work for the annual auction of the New Hampshire Furniture Masters Association.

Dean Powell ("A Meditation on the Desk," page 72, and elsewhere throughout this book) is a professional photographer in Lowell, Massachusetts, who has specialized in studio furniture for more than twenty years.

Kathran Siegel ("Art Furniture," page 84) maintains a studio in Bucks County, Pennsylvania. Her interest in furniture design is part of a larger interest in contemporary lifestyle, for which she finds expression in a variety of mediums and formats. Siegel also teaches art and design courses at a number of colleges in the Philadelphia area.

Phone: 434-973-1488
Fax: 434-973-0336
www.furnituresociety.org

First
Class
Stamp

The Furniture Society
Box 18
Free Union, VA 22940

Phone: 434-973-1488
Fax: 434-973-0336
www.furnituresociety.org

Send this form with membership fee to:

The Furniture Society
Box 18
Free Union, VA 22940